TRUE NORTH CABIN COOKBOOK

TRUE NORTH CABIN COOKBOOK

Stephanie Hansen

RECIPES & STORIES FROM A NORTH WOODS TABLE

MINNESOTA HISTORICAL SOCIETY PRESS

To Kurt, Ellie, and Dolores

*and to all my extended family,
friends, and fellow foodies*

mnhspress.org

The Minnesota Historical Society Press is a member of the Association of University Presses.

Manufactured in Canada

10 9 8 7 6 5 4 3 2

♾ The paper used in this publication meets the minimum requirements of the American National Standard for Information Sciences — Permanence for Printed Library Materials, ANSI Z39.48-1984.

International Standard Book Number

ISBN: 978-1-68134-235-1 (hardcover)

Library of Congress Cataloging-in-Publication Data

Names: Hansen, Stephanie, author.

Title: True North cabin cookbook : recipes and stories from a north woods table / Stephanie Hansen.

Description: St. Paul, MN : Minnesota Historical Society Press, [2022] | Includes index.

Identifiers: LCCN 2022010079 | ISBN 9781681342351 (hardcover)

Subjects: LCSH: Cooking. | Quick and easy cooking. | Seasonal cooking. | Summer. | LCGFT: Cookbooks.

Classification: LCC TX652 .H3625 2022 | DDC 641.5 — dc23/eng/20220318

LC record available at https://lccn.loc.gov/2022010079

True North Cabin Cookbook was designed and set in type by Susan Everson in St. Paul, Minnesota.
The typefaces are Montebello, Rockeby, MultipleSlab, and MultipleSans.

TRUE NORTH CABIN COOKBOOK

CABIN COOKING

2   True North Island is my husband's family property on Burntside Lake near Ely, Minnesota. It's somewhat remote: twenty miles as the crow flies from the Canadian border, one lake portage from the Boundary Waters Canoe Area, and two miles by boat from the marina at Burntside Lodge.

The island cabin is small, with two bedrooms, a living room, and combination kitchen and dining room. The kitchen is not glamorous — there are no marble countertops, no center island, no pantry, no dishwasher, no disposal, no microwave (there's just no room), and the kind of propane stove found in small RVs or hunting shacks. We do not have a spectacular brick pizza oven out on the patio, and our idea of an outdoor kitchen is a Weber grill with one side burner (we gave up on charcoal long ago, after almost burning down the island with two-day-old embers — see page 101).

We pump water out of the lake for washing dishes, showering, boiling noodles, and making coffee. For drinking water, we drive our Lund boat down the lake to a portage where we fill up gallon jugs from a natural spring. But I'll be honest: the island does have electricity, and I do have a blender, an ice cream maker, and even a food processor. So cabin cooking is not camping cooking or even "glamping" cooking. Our family is not grilling over a wood fire, eating freeze-dried anything, or attempting to make everything in one pot on a single burner.

What we don't have at the island is access to specialty food markets. We do have Zup's grocery store in the small town of Ely. Zup's is a family-owned market founded in 1916 by "Grandpa" John Zupancich. Grandpa was originally a sausage maker, and to this day the store offers house-made smoked Polish sausage, bacon, liverwurst, bratwurst, sauerkraut (of course), porchetta, and much more. They cater to the three thousand local residents year-round, but also to seasonal cabin owners like us. They carry a wide selection of foods, and their meats are very, very good. So, for the purposes of this cookbook, if you can't find

the ingredients at Zup's, then we don't cook it. Theoretically, you can pick up any ingredients called for on these pages at your local grocery store.

We also don't have access to the fresh fruits and vegetables found at the huge farmers' markets located in the Twin Cities. But we do have our small garden, where we cultivate vegetables suitable for northern Minnesota's short growing season: fresh lettuces, onions, garlic, asparagus, Early Girl tomatoes, zucchini, rhubarb, cucumbers, peas, carrots, beets, turnips, and occasionally eggplant. On our deck that overlooks the lake are pots with fresh herbs like thyme, oregano, chives, basil, and rosemary. We also have the vast woods of Superior National Forest, where we forage fresh blueberries, raspberries, and strawberries and wild mushrooms like morels and shiitakes. If you don't have access to some of these ingredients, just make do as best you can, and if you don't have a pot of fresh herbs on your deck or patio, by all means plant one — fresh herbs can really elevate a dish.

We prepare our meals with simple cookware. I will not be cutting corners with an Instant Pot or air fryer (though I do love these kitchen tools and use them throughout winter at home in Minneapolis). For frying we have our grandmother's cast iron deep fryer, and we cook our meat in the oven, in a cast iron skillet, or preferably on the grill. A robin's-egg blue Le Creuset Dutch oven made its way to the island via my mother-in-law, Dolores. Our one luxury is the first Cuisinart food processor we ever owned, given to us as a wedding present over twenty-five years ago by island neighbors Harry and Lila Jacob.

I could say that cabin cooking is about simply prepared meals made with fresh ingredients purchased locally, but I think, more importantly, cabin cooking is about the recipes our family has shared over my thirty years on Burntside Lake. These tasty meals throughout the summer are the heart of our daily cabin life. I'm so excited to share them with you.

THE DUTCH OVEN

When I first met Kurt in 1989, I was dancing on tabletops at a nightclub. This is not to imply anything untoward. I worked as a cocktail waitress at Heartthrob Café in downtown St. Paul. During the day, Heartthrob was a back-to-the-fifties restaurant that served phenomenal juicy burgers and old-fashioned milkshakes and malts. The food was delivered to each table by servers festooned with buttons and suspenders who swept across the linoleum floor on roller skates. Then, every twenty minutes, a doo-wop or Motown song would come on the jukebox, and the servers would stop what they were doing to perform a prepared dance routine. In the evening, the nightclub on the other side of a vast wall would open with a DJ and a dance floor. I worked at the nightclub side of Heartthrob. Instead of the demure bowling shirts and ankle-length poodle skirts worn in the restaurant, the cocktail waitresses wore leotard tops with hot pink poodle skirts that fell considerably above the knee. There was no way we could move through a packed nightclub with roller skates, so we wore practical high-top Reebok tennis shoes. Then, when our dance songs played, all of us, including the bartenders, barbacks, doormen, and managers, would climb up on the tables and bar tops and do our choreographed routines. This is where I met Kurt. He was the manager.

Kurt had just been hired at Heartthrob. Before he arrived, all we knew about our new manager was that he'd worked at nightclubs in Las Vegas. We expected some slick Vegas guy with shiny hair, a silk shirt, and gold finger rings. What we got was a preppy-looking kid with horn-rimmed tortoiseshell glasses, khaki pants, and a button-down pressed cotton shirt. I thought he looked cute. Then, when I got to know him, I found out he'd grown up in Minneapolis. And that his family owned an island near the Canadian border.

One thing led to another. Managers, of course, were not supposed to date their employees — even then. I unabashedly asked him out for coffee, and he declined. I stayed past closing time, and as with every bar I've ever worked in, when the shift ended and the doors were locked, the staff sat around and had a few beers or shots of Rumple Minze. I brought a beer into Kurt's office, where he was finishing up the ledgers, and we talked. I talked about growing up in Bloomington, my divorced parents, and school at the University of Minnesota. Kurt talked about growing up in south Minneapolis, summers on Burntside Lake, and the nightclub business, with wild stories of Las Vegas. A few days later, he did have coffee with me at Muddy Waters on Lyndale Avenue. After that we ignored the corporate rules and secretly went on a first date. He took me to the old Uptown Bar, across the street from the brand-new Calhoun Square mall. We stood in back and listened to some band like Babes in Toyland or the Flamin' Oh's. I can't remember who because I was focused on him. Then he did something odd — and I guess sweet or proper: he asked if he could kiss me. Well . . .

That was on a rare Thursday when both of us had the night off. We also had the following Sunday and Monday off. That Saturday evening while both of us were doing our jobs and dancing on tabletops, Kurt asked if I'd like to spend the next two days at his family's island cabin, sans family. He said we could drive up right after work. I had only the change of clothes that I came to work in — no toiletries or toothbrush — but I said, "Sure." My first visit to True North Island started when we took off at 1 a.m. from St. Paul and arrived in complete darkness in Ely at 4:30 a.m.

So here I was, twenty years old, taking off in the middle of the night with a nightclub manager whom I'd known for maybe three weeks, who was ten years my senior. We'd had coffee and one date. We drove nearly four hours into the middle of nowhere; I'd never been farther north than Brainerd. We got into a fishing boat and crossed a remote lake in near darkness with fog on the water. We arrived at a dock — God only knows how he found it in the dark — and tied up the boat. We walked along a path to what, in the dim light, looked like a brown shack. It was May and cold and windy. I wore jeans, a brown leather jacket, and my eighties white cowboy boots with fringe. He unlocked a bolted door and it creaked open. I entered the complete darkness of this remote cabin with a man behind me. Even now, after all these years, it still sounds like the opening scene of a slasher movie.

Then he turned on the lights (thank God the island had electricity). It was no shack, but no palace either. The living room had a few chairs and a couch pointed toward a fireplace, and Kurt started a fire to warm us up. There were two small bedrooms, a bathroom with a toilet we weren't supposed to use, a kitchen with butcher block counters, and a dining area with a maple table and four chairs. The floors were varnished pine boards, the walls tongue and groove cedar. There was an outhouse tucked in the woods somewhere, but for that morning I just held it. The cabin warmed up, Kurt put on a record — Willie Nelson's *Stardust* — and we snuggled in. In retrospect, maybe it was a poor decision to go with Kurt into the north woods after knowing him only a few weeks, but it turned out *not* to be a scene from a slasher movie.

It wasn't until we woke up around noon that I could see the whole island. Surrounding the cabin was a cedar deck that nearly matched the square footage of our first house (still ten years in the future). From the deck you could see the lake in every direction. The trees were all mature white and Norwegian pine that stacked up like matchsticks. Beyond the water were more islands, some with trees and some just bare granite rock like the backs of giant whales. A half mile distant was the mainland shore, and I could just make out a few other cabins. Otherwise, there was not a boat or soul out on the lake. I was shown the outhouse. I had never been in an outhouse, but it turned out to be very self-explanatory, and it was clean.

In the afternoon we took the small fishing boat across the lake to where we started the night before. What I hadn't seen in the darkness was the boat slip, one of ten, sided with split logs painted a burnt orange beneath a long, green roof. This was the marina at Burntside Lodge. The lodge itself, built in 1921 and on the National Register of Historic Places, was on a hill a short distance from the marina. In years to come, the lodge would be a place to celebrate birthdays and our wedding anniversary in June. But that day in May, before the fishing opener, the lodge was closed. We drove into the town of Ely and bought groceries at Zup's supermarket, where months later I discovered their delicious smoked meats and fish. Kurt loaded the grocery cart with enough food for lunch and two home-cooked dinners. I bought a toothbrush and magazines.

didn't start off my life in the kitchen. My mother was a stay-at-home mom, and she cooked all our meals. She wasn't a fancy cook, but she was a good cook. *Better Homes and Gardens* and Betty Crocker were her guides, which was probably typical for those times, when you'd be hard pressed to find an artichoke in a grocery store, let alone anchovy paste or fancy mushrooms. My mother cooked staples like meat loaf coated with ketchup and sloppy joes with Campbell's chicken gumbo soup as the base. She pan fried her own chicken and made liberal use of elbow macaroni in casseroles, chili, and homemade mac and cheese (find her recipe on page 104). I also had two older sisters who were always there to help in the kitchen and do dishes while I watched the latest episode of *The Brady Bunch*. I was lazy, and my sisters did all the heavy lifting in the kitchen. My only job was to clean the banister in the front hall with a feather duster. As I grew up and my parents divorced, my mother went back to work. I ate lots of toast and cereal, and my idea of cooking was microwaved popcorn. So, frankly, I was surprised that Kurt cooked.

He'd grown up differently, a mama's boy who always helped in the kitchen, with a mom who watched Julia Child and had an original copy of *Mastering the Art of French Cooking*. Kurt had drifted into the nightclub business after first working stints at 510 Groveland Haute Cuisine and Rudolph's Bar-B-Que. Kurt knew how to cook, and that afternoon on the island he began mixing flour, salt, and yeast for French bread, then sliced a chuck steak into cubes for beef bourguignon. I drank cheap red wine and watched him cook, absolutely smitten.

He started with a cast iron Dutch oven, a heavy and deep five-quart pot with a lid. The cubed steak was dredged in flour with salt and pepper, then browned in olive oil using the Dutch oven. The meat was set aside, and he sautéed garlic and julienned carrots. Once those were lightly cooked, the meat was added back in, along with fresh thyme, tablespoons of tomato paste, and half the bottle of wine I was drinking. The Dutch oven was covered and shoved into the small cabin oven to cook for hours. All afternoon the oven heated the cabin and filled it with a deep, rich aroma. The bread dough rose in the heat, and later Kurt rolled out twin loaves that were left to stand and rise again on the stove top, covered with a flour sack kitchen towel his grandmother had embroidered. Toward evening, the Dutch oven and the loaves switched places, and while the bread baked, he sautéed pearl onions and mushrooms. Those were added to the Dutch oven, which was then moved back into the oven to finish.

The beef bourguignon was my first meal with this man on an island in northern Minnesota, a place I learned to love and cherish over the years. We ate at the small kitchen table with more red wine and lots of butter for the bread. The beef stew came out thick and fragrant, with meat that melted in my mouth. The loaves were as thin as my wrist, with a stiff crust and light and airy insides. We ate bowls of the stew, then sopped up the gravy with hunks of buttered bread. This turned out to be the recipe I started with a few years later when I caught the cooking bug and began to take over our kitchen. I learned that it wasn't the classic Julia Child recipe, but close to it — and good enough given the meager resources in Ely and for a remote island in the middle of a sprawling lake.

The next day we took out the fishing boat and trolled slowly up a river, the Dead River, to its headwaters at Twin Lakes. The ice had just gone out, but already the marshes surrounding the river were teeming with life. Beavers slapped their tails as we moved near; ahead of us were two trumpeter swans that danced away, slapping their feet against the water as they gained elevation and flew farther down the river. In the distance we saw a cow moose standing in two feet of water and eating willows. Kurt showed me a pitcher plant that had bloomed into a purple and green sac-like thing with a mouth that attracted bugs, which the plant apparently ate. In one of the Twin Lakes, we had a picnic of Brie cheese and leftover bread, along with more red wine. We took naps when we got back to the island and played cards later in the afternoon.

That night Kurt made penne alfredo with sausage and peppers (recipe on page 16), a dish he learned from a cook at a restaurant in Las Vegas. It's still one of my favorites. I watched as he boiled the pasta until al dente, then kept it hot with a splash of olive oil. In a cast iron skillet, he cooked spiced Italian sausage with garlic, sliced onions, red peppers, and peeled and diced tomatoes, then added two cups of heavy cream. He slid his spatula along the sides of the skillet to keep the cream from boiling over. When the cream had reduced to a consistency that coated the spatula, he added the hot pasta. He mixed in grated Parmesan cheese to thicken the sauce further and then sprinkled fresh chopped parsley over the top. He served the pasta with a salad dressed with just lemon, olive oil, salt, and pepper — a light crispness that cut the heaviness of the pasta. That night we switched from red wine to a Chardonnay from California. Afterward, I helped him hand wash the dishes.

The next morning, we drove back to the Twin Cities, our jobs, and the clandestine romance we continued until we were ultimately discovered. By then we didn't much care.

To me, preparing a meal from scratch is about breaking bread and making friends. Every great salesperson knows the power of breaking bread. Get the client out for an expensive meal at an exquisite restaurant, drink martinis and wine, talk about movies, families, and sports over medium-rare steaks, creamed spinach, and baked russet potatoes, then delve into the deal over coffee, cognac, and chocolate soufflé. It's a sure thing. I enjoy cooking and serving food because I can create new friendships, and it brings me closer to the people I love.

Two years after we met, I bought my own Dutch oven, a five-quart Le Creuset with black enameled cast iron. I cooked my first beef bourguignon directly from Julia Child's *Mastering the Art of French Cooking.* I went to the local butcher and asked for lardons, and she cut me thick slices of bacon without smirking. I bought fresh pearl onions where Kurt had used frozen, and I carefully peeled and crosscut each one. I used shiitake mushrooms that, in later years, I would find wild in the woods around Ely. I used an expensive bottle of red Bordeaux for the sauce when I should have used cheap Burgundy. I bought a loaf of the best French bread from New French Café. At the time, while Kurt was back at school getting his master's degree in business, we were living three blocks from the Minneapolis Institute of Art in a double bungalow next to the thirty-foot sound barrier bordering I-35W. I was working at the *Twin Cities Reader* selling classified ads, and we could barely afford the chuck steak, let alone the Bordeaux I carelessly wasted on the sauce. I served the bourguignon in my new Le Creuset, and the two of us filled our wine glasses with the rest of the Bordeaux and reminisced about our first meal on True North Island. Our first night on the island, that opening scene from a slasher movie, had turned into a lifelong love affair.

Cocktails

Cocktails on True North island are served at 6 p.m. sharp after everyone has taken a nap and cleaned up with a sauna and a swim. No matter what the weather was like all day, during the golden hour the wind seems to die down and the pontoon boats come out for cocktail cruises on the lake. I keep a well-stocked bar at the cabin, and I usually like to start off happy hour with a seasonal signature cocktail. Being on the deck surrounded by water makes cocktails at Burntside a relaxing precursor to the meal-time ritual.

Rhubarb Syrup

Makes about 1 cup

Toward the end of May, I start to harvest the rhubarb grown in our Hilltop Garden. The garden is across the lake on a parcel husband Kurt and I bought from a Craigslist ad in 2016. We had always wanted a piece of property on shore so we could visit during the fall, winter, and spring seasons when the island is closed. The one-bedroom shore cabin located high on a hilltop also serves as overflow for island guests in the summer — we call it Hilltop. In 2018 we started the large Hilltop vegetable garden. True North island itself is rocky, dirt-starved, and shaded by a canopy of pines, with no viable spot for a garden.

One of the first things I planted in the Hilltop Garden was rhubarb so I could make my own rhubarb syrup for cocktails. Rhubarb stalks can be quickly turned into a syrup that enhances the first gin and tonics of the season (why wait for Memorial Day?). The leftover rhubarb solids make a rough jam that's great on toast or a muffin or swirled into the batter of a quick bread recipe.

4 cups chopped rhubarb

1 cup granulated sugar

1 cup water

Combine the rhubarb, sugar, and water in a saucepan and bring to a boil. Lower the heat to simmer, stirring occasionally, until the fruit is soft, about 15 minutes.

Set a mesh strainer over a large bowl. Pour the mixture through the strainer and press the solids with the back of a spatula to extract more syrup. Carefully pour the syrup into a clean bottle or Mason jar. Cover and refrigerate.

French 75

Serves 1

This is a favorite cocktail to celebrate that first day of vacation up on True North Island.

1 ounce gin (Solveig Gin from Far North Spirits in Hallock, Minnesota)

½ ounce fresh lemon juice

½ ounce simple syrup (see tip)

3 ounces champagne (or other sparkling wine like cava or prosecco)

lemon twist, for garnish

Add the gin, lemon juice, and simple syrup to a shaker with ice and shake until well chilled. Strain into a champagne flute. Top with champagne. Garnish with a lemon twist.

TIP: Make a simple syrup by boiling equal parts sugar and water until the sugar dissolves.

Champagne Cocktail

Serves 1

I love champagne, cava, and prosecco, and I typically have a few bottles on hand at the cabin. I drink bubbles for special occasions, but I also enjoy cocktails with bubbles. A simple glass of cava mixed with a raspberry shrub or a few drops of cherry vanilla bitters can feel really fancy and elevate any gathering. The simple champagne cocktail is always welcome at a party and is a signature cocktail I often serve to my lady friends.

1 sugar cube

2 dashes bitters (Bittercube Jamaican No. 2 or Angostura)

champagne (or other sparkling wine like cava or prosecco), to top

lemon twist, for garnish

Drop a sugar cube into a chilled champagne flute or similar glass. Add bitters onto the sugar cube. Fill the glass with champagne or other sparkling wine. Garnish with a lemon twist.

Rhubarb Gin & Tonic

Serves 1

2 ounces gin (Vikre Boreal Spruce Gin from Duluth, Minnesota)

2 tablespoons Rhubarb Syrup (page 11)

tonic water (Q or Fever-Tree)

fresh rosemary or thyme sprigs, for garnish

In a rocks glass filled with ice, combine gin and rhubarb syrup. Top with tonic water. Garnish with fresh thyme or rosemary.

Ruby Red Grapefruit Margaritas

Serves 8

Margaritas are always in season on the island. There is something about a margarita that whispers relaxation and cabin time. This recipe calls for fresh-squeezed ruby red grapefruit juice or the store-bought variety (I like Simply Grapefruit brand). If you prefer a spicy version, float thin slices of jalapeño on top.

2½ cups blanco tequila

1 cup Cointreau or Triple Sec or other orange liqueur

2½ cups fresh ruby red grapefruit juice

1 cup fresh lime juice (about 8 limes)

8 teaspoons Tajín (see tip) or kosher salt, to rim the glasses

1 lime, to rim the glasses, plus 1 lime, sliced, for garnish

Pour tequila, Cointreau, and juices into a pitcher and stir.

Pour Tajín onto a saucer. Rub a cut lime around the rim of each glass and spin the glass in the Tajín to coat the rim.

Pour mixed cocktail over ice in glasses with Tajín rims, and garnish each with a lime slice.

TIP: This chili-lime spice is available in the specialty spice section of your grocery store.

Beef Bourguignon

Serves 6-8

This version is adapted from Julia Child's *Mastering the Art of French Cooking.*

1 tablespoon extra-virgin olive oil

8 slices bacon, roughly chopped

3 pounds chuck steak, cut into 2-inch cubes

1 teaspoon kosher salt

1 teaspoon freshly ground coarse black pepper

2 tablespoons all-purpose flour

1 carrot, cut into ½-inch rounds

1 white onion, finely chopped

4 cloves garlic, minced or grated

2 teaspoons finely chopped fresh thyme leaves

3 cups red wine (a hardy, inexpensive Chianti or Burgundy — good enough to drink while cooking)

3 cups beef stock or beef consommé

3 tablespoons tomato paste

3 tablespoons butter

1 pound fresh mushrooms (white button, portobello, or shiitake), quartered

1 (14- to 16-ounce) bag frozen small pearl onions, thawed

2 tablespoons finely chopped fresh parsley

egg noodles or mashed potatoes, for serving

Heat oven to 350 degrees. In a large Dutch oven or heavy-bottomed, ovenproof pot set over medium heat, add oil and cook the bacon, stirring often, for about 5 minutes, until crisp and browned. When the bacon is crisp, use a slotted spoon to transfer it to a paper towel–lined plate and set aside. Leave the bacon fat in the pot.

Pat beef dry with a paper towel, then place beef into a zip-top bag with salt, pepper, and flour. Shake to coat. Working in batches, sear the flour-coated beef in the bacon fat over medium-high heat, about 4-5 minutes, until pieces are browned on all sides. (This step browns the flour and covers the meat with a light crust.)

In the remaining fat, cook the carrots and onions, stirring often, until softened, about 3 minutes; then add the garlic and thyme and cook for 1 minute. Drain any excess fat and return the bacon and beef to the pot; season with salt and pepper.

Add wine and stock to submerge the meat. Stir in the tomato paste. Cover and bring to a boil on the stove top. Then place the covered pot in the lower third of the preheated oven. Cook for 2½ hours.

In the last 10 minutes of cooking time, heat the butter in a medium skillet, then add the mushrooms. Cook for about 3 minutes, shaking the pan occasionally to coat mushrooms with butter. Add thawed pearl onions and cook for 2 minutes more. Mushrooms should be slightly browned, and onions heated through. Add mixture to the Dutch oven, stirring to combine. Cover and return to the oven for 15 more minutes.

Garnish with parsley and serve with egg noodles or mashed potatoes.

Farfalle Alfredo Pepper and Sausage Pasta

Serves 4

My hungry husband turned his fettuccine alfredo into a complete family-style meal. He produced a version of this recipe while on a ski trip to Colorado. After being out on the slopes all day, the last thing anyone wanted to do was cook an elaborate meal or make the effort to go out to a restaurant. We just wanted food — hot, hearty, carbo-loading food. His first pass with this recipe had been with fettuccine noodles, but over time farfalle seemed to work better, with the pasta distributing evenly among the ingredients and holding sauce in its crinkled bows. This quick, family-style recipe offers maximum calories for those who have been enjoying the outdoors all day. Feel free to spice it up with a dash of Cajun spices.

12 ounces farfalle pasta (penne works well too)

2 tablespoons extra-virgin olive oil

1 pound sweet Italian sausage, casings removed, crumbled

½ cup finely chopped onion

½ cup finely chopped red bell pepper

3 cloves garlic, minced

1 (14.5-ounce) can diced tomatoes, drained

1 cup heavy cream

½ teaspoon kosher salt

½ cup freshly grated Parmesan cheese

1 teaspoon black pepper

Cook pasta according to package instructions until tender. Meanwhile, heat oil in a large, heavy skillet over medium heat. Add sausage, onions, red pepper, and garlic. Cook until sausage is no longer pink and onions are translucent, stirring frequently. Add tomatoes, cream, and salt, and simmer until mixture thickens slightly. Add pasta to the skillet, tossing to combine. Stir in Parmesan cheese and pepper.

Kurt's Caesar Salad

Serves 4-6

My husband, Kurt, worked for a few years at the once famous but now extinct Las Vegas restaurant Andre's. Back then, French dining still included recipes of rich food adapted by Auguste Escoffier in his *Le Guide Culinaire*, and many dishes, including the Caesar salad, were assembled tableside. This recipe is based on Escoffier's classic and includes only lemon as the acid and all those gooey things that you don't have to tell your kids or guests about (like raw egg yolks and anchovy paste). You will need a half cup of dressing and two cups of croutons. Feel free to make a double or triple batch of dressing and croutons so you have leftovers for another salad.

For dressing
2 large egg yolks

2 cloves garlic, minced or grated

1 teaspoon Dijon mustard

1 tablespoon anchovy paste

½ cup extra-virgin olive oil

2 tablespoons fresh lemon juice

¼ cup finely grated Parmesan cheese

½ teaspoon kosher salt

freshly ground black pepper

For croutons
4 cups hearty bread cut into 1-inch cubes

¼ cup extra-virgin olive oil

1 teaspoon salt

6 grinds freshly cracked black pepper

For salad
¼ cup finely grated Parmesan cheese, plus more for serving

2 heads romaine lettuce, chopped into 1-inch pieces

anchovy fillets, optional

lemon wedge, for garnish

For dressing
Blend the egg yolks, garlic, mustard, and anchovy paste in a food processor, then slowly add the olive oil. The mixture will start to thicken into an aioli; stop the food processor before it gets too thick. Add lemon juice and Parmesan cheese and mix until just blended. Add salt and pepper to taste.

For croutons
Heat oven to 350 degrees. In a large bowl, toss cubed bread with olive oil until evenly coated. Add salt and pepper and toss to distribute. Arrange croutons on a large baking sheet. Bake for about 8 minutes; flip bread pieces with a spatula to redistribute, and cook 7 minutes more, until golden and crispy.

To assemble
Place ½ cup dressing in the base of a large wooden salad bowl. Add Parmesan cheese, chopped romaine, and 2 cups croutons. Toss until well combined. Serve with an optional anchovy fillet on top, additional cheese, or a lemon wedge for garnish.

Stephanie's Grilled Caesar Salad

Serves 4

I understand that grilling salad might seem a little weird, but trust me on this. The slight char caramelizes the salad and brings out the sweetness. The warmth enhances the dressing drizzled over the top, and the presentation of the half hearts of romaine gives a real wow factor next to grilled lamb or steak or by themselves on a beautiful platter with grilled half lemons.

8 (½-inch-thick) baguette slices

½ cup extra-virgin olive oil, divided

2 lemons, cut in half vertically

2 hearts romaine, sliced in half horizontally

4 tablespoons Kurt's Caesar Salad dressing (page 17)

¼ cup Parmesan cheese shaved with a vegetable peeler

Lightly brush both sides of baguette slices with olive oil and grill until there are brown charred lines on the bread, about 3 minutes per side. Set aside.

Brush olive oil on cut sides of lemon halves and lay flesh side down on the grill until they are brown with some charred areas, about 4–5 minutes.

Brush olive oil on the romaine halves and grill until there are some charred leaves, 4–5 minutes.

To assemble the salad, on a pretty platter arrange the grilled romaine with charred lemons around the edge. Top with 2 baguette slices per romaine half. Drizzle 1 tablespoon dressing on each romaine half, and sprinkle shaved Parmesan cheese on top. Serve warm.

White Bean Tuna Salad

Serves 2 for lunch

Having cans of food on the island throughout the summer minimizes the number of long and complicated trips to Zup's grocery store. To get to the store, we first get in and untie the "blue boat," an aluminum Lund fishing boat, which is our main source of transportation to and from the island. We drive eight minutes across the lake, which can be windy, choppy, rainy, or otherwise uncomfortable, to the long, burnt-orange boathouse at Burntside Lodge, built in 1920 with ten islander stalls. From there we get into the car and drive twelve minutes into town to Zup's. As you can see, a grocery run — no matter how small — is at least an hour round trip. Having cans of tomatoes, tuna, and beans and plenty of rice and pasta on hand is key to a successful island stay. This salad has become an easy family favorite when no one wants to "run" to the store.

2 teaspoons lemon zest

3 tablespoons fresh lemon juice

3 tablespoons extra-virgin olive oil

1 clove garlic, minced or grated

1 teaspoon Dijon mustard

1 teaspoon kosher salt

freshly ground black pepper, to taste

1 (15-ounce) can cannellini (white) beans, rinsed and drained

¼ cup chopped red onion

¼ cup chopped green onions, green parts only

3 tablespoons chopped fresh parsley

3 tablespoons chopped fresh dill

1 (6-ounce) can chunk light tuna in oil, drained

Whisk lemon zest, lemon juice, oil, garlic, mustard, salt, and pepper in a medium bowl. Add beans, red onion, green onions, parsley, and dill, then flake in tuna by hand. Toss to coat well.

Greek Salad with Quinoa

Serves 4

This salad has a funny backstory. My daughter graduated from the University of Minnesota in the spring of 2021. We were just getting through the first round of COVID-19 vaccines and feeling like we could gather to celebrate with friends and family. I came up with a menu for a brunch buffet that I thought was fantastic and emailed it to Ellie. The menu included kale salad, quiche, a vegetable tart, a charcuterie platter, lemon poppy seed bread, blueberry bread pudding, and Greek quinoa salad. After a few days with no reply, I called her. She said, "Mom, where are the breakfast items? You know, like French toast, bacon, hash browns, donuts . . . you know, *breakfast food*. No offense, Mom, but nobody wants kale salad and Greek quinoa salad for brunch, no matter how delicious it is." So I reshaped the menu to add more breakfast items, but the Greek quinoa salad stayed. The day of the party, I had no fewer than three requests for the recipe because it was so delicious. Ellie and I still laugh about it to this day.

For vinaigrette

½ cup extra-virgin olive oil

⅓ cup fresh lemon juice

2 cloves garlic, minced or grated

1 teaspoon Dijon mustard

1 teaspoon kosher salt

1 teaspoon freshly ground
  black pepper

For salad

1½ cups water

1 tablespoon extra-virgin olive oil

1 cup dried quinoa

4 small Persian cucumbers, halved
  and sliced, or 1 large seedless
  cucumber, cut lengthwise and
  then into half-moons

1 pint grape tomatoes, halved

1 cup kalamata olives, pitted
  and halved

¼ cup chopped red onion

¼ cup chopped green onions, light
  green and white parts

1 cup crumbled feta cheese

¼ cup chopped parsley, plus parsley
  sprigs for garnish

¼ cup chopped mint, plus mint sprigs
  for garnish

For vinaigrette

Whisk together olive oil, lemon juice, garlic, mustard, salt, and pepper until well combined.

For salad

In a medium saucepan, combine water and olive oil and bring to a boil. Add quinoa, stirring to mix, then remove from heat. Cover and let sit for 3 minutes, until water has been absorbed. Fluff with a fork to separate the grains of quinoa. Transfer to a large bowl to cool to room temperature.

To the cooled quinoa, add the cucumber, tomatoes, olives, red onion, green onions, crumbled feta, parsley, and mint. Drizzle with vinaigrette. Toss until well combined. Garnish with parsley or mint sprigs when serving.

Soup

French Onion Soup

My Twin Cities friends affectionately call me "the soup lady." I make soup and freeze it in Mason jars throughout the year (be sure to leave 1½ inches of airspace between soup and lid before freezing). Soup is such a warm, comforting dish, and it makes great use of leftovers in your refrigerator or dribs and drabs of garden vegetables left in the crisper. At the cabin there's a plastic bag in the freezer that everyone knows is the "stock" bag. I put potato peels, kale stems, onion tops, meat scraps, and bones in the stock bag, and about once a month I make stock. I usually make chicken stock or vegetable stock, but sometimes I make a lamb broth specifically for my dog, Nikki. When the wind is blowing cold from the north and whipping the waves into whitecaps, it's comforting to have a pot of soup on the stove and a loaf of bread in the oven.

Serves 4–6

½ cup (1 stick) unsalted butter

6 large sweet onions (about 5 pounds), cut into ¼-inch-thick slices

5 cups beef broth (or substitute chicken broth or vegetable broth)

2 cans beef consommé (Campbell's)

2 teaspoons Worcestershire sauce

2 bay leaves

3 sprigs fresh thyme

1 baguette, cut into ½-inch-thick slices

3 tablespoons extra-virgin olive oil

1 teaspoon kosher salt

1 teaspoon freshly cracked black pepper

1½ cups shredded Gruyère cheese, divided

In a large stockpot or Dutch oven over medium-low heat, melt the butter. When the butter begins to foam, add the onions, tossing to coat. The onions will cook and caramelize slowly on medium-low heat. Stir the onions every 15 minutes. They are done when they are richly brown and sweet, about 45 minutes. Add the beef broth, beef consommé, Worcestershire sauce, bay leaves, and thyme. Simmer for another 45 minutes.

While the soup simmers, heat oven to 350 degrees. Brush the tops of the baguette slices with olive oil and bake for about 5 minutes to toast. Set aside. Increase the oven temperature to 450 degrees.

Remove the bay leaves and thyme stems from the soup. Season to taste with salt and pepper. Ladle the warm soup into ovenproof bowls. Top each bowl with 1 or 2 baguette slices. Top baguette slices with ¼ cup Gruyère cheese per bowl and bake until the cheese melts and begins to bubble and brown.

Creamy Kale, Sausage, and Potato Soup

Serves 8

This recipe uses the Slovenian smoked polish sausages from Zup's, the local grocery store in Ely. You could also choose any favorite smoked sausage.

2 tablespoons extra-virgin olive oil

1 yellow onion, chopped

4 cloves garlic, minced

1½ pounds Yukon Gold potatoes, quartered and cut into ¼- to ½-inch chunks

4 cups finely chopped kale (see tip)

8 cups (2 quarts) chicken broth

1 teaspoon smoked paprika

4 Zup's smoked polish sausages, cut into ¼-inch slices

1 (15-ounce) can cannellini (white) beans, drained

⅓ cup heavy cream

2 teaspoons kosher salt

freshly cracked black pepper, to taste

zest of 1 lemon

¼ cup fresh lemon juice

Place a large pot or Dutch oven over medium heat. Add the oil, onions, and garlic, and cook, stirring, for 3 minutes. Next add the potatoes, kale, broth, and smoked paprika to the pot. Bring to a boil, then lower the heat. Cover and simmer for 20 minutes to soften the potatoes and kale. Stir in the sliced sausage, beans, and heavy cream. Simmer for 5 more minutes. Finish it off by stirring in the salt, pepper, lemon zest, and lemon juice.

TIP: I like lacinato kale, but you can also use curly kale, spinach, beet greens, or collard greens. On the island we make do with whatever greens we have.

Roasted Chicken Pot Pie

Serves 6–8

Like most kids from my generation, I grew up on Swanson Chicken Pot Pie. It was a treat, usually on Fridays when my parents were out for the night and my eldest sister had to babysit. While my sister talked on the phone to her boyfriend or on the party line, we cooked Totino's Pizza Rolls or chicken pot pie — which I liked the best. My tastes evolved from that experience into meeting friends on Christmas Eve at the Lexington restaurant in St. Paul. Their version of chicken pot pie was slightly more sophisticated than Swanson's, with just a top crust over a crock filled with chunks of chicken breast and sliced vegetables in a creamy gravy. This recipe is an hours-long cooking project (perfect for a cold, rainy day) but it takes the pot pie up a notch with the flavors of roasted chicken mingled with caramelized vegetables that have been stewed in their own juices. And though the recipe may take longer to prepare, it's surprisingly simple, and much of the time involves waiting for the mélange to roast.

For crust

1¼ cups all-purpose flour

1 teaspoon kosher salt

1 cup (2 sticks) high-fat, unsalted butter, chilled and cut into ½-inch cubes

3 tablespoons ice water

1 tablespoon vodka

For filling

6 tablespoons unsalted butter

1 large onion, finely chopped

2 medium carrots, peeled and cut crosswise into ¼-inch pieces

1 medium parsnip, peeled and cut crosswise into ¼-inch pieces

1 medium russet potato, peeled and cut crosswise into ¼-inch pieces

4 cloves garlic, minced

6 tablespoons all-purpose flour

¼ cup water

4 cups (1 quart) chicken stock

½ cup 2 percent milk

4 cups roasted chicken, torn into bite-size pieces (see tip)

1 cup frozen peas

2 teaspoons chopped fresh thyme leaves

3 tablespoons finely chopped fresh Italian flat-leaf parsley

1 tablespoon kosher salt

1 teaspoon black pepper

1 large egg

TIP: See Roasted Chicken with Thyme and Lemon, page 34; or use store-bought rotisserie chicken.

For crust

In bowl of a food processor, pulse flour and salt 2 to 3 times until combined. Scatter cubed butter over flour and pulse 4 to 5 times, until flour is evenly distributed. (Dough should look crumbly.) Add 3 tablespoons ice water through the food processor tube, pulsing once after each addition. The crumbs should begin to form larger clusters. Add the vodka and continue to pulse until the dough comes together in a ball and awkwardly spins in the machine.

Remove dough from bowl and place in a mound on a clean surface. Work the dough just enough to form a ball. Press into a disk and wrap with plastic wrap; refrigerate for at least 1 hour and up to 2 days.

For filling

In a Dutch oven over medium-high heat, melt the butter. Add the onions and cook for about 3 minutes, until soft. Add carrots, parsnips, and potato, and cook for 3 minutes. Add garlic and cook, stirring, 1 more minute, then stir in the flour. Cook for about 5 minutes, stirring constantly to coat the vegetables in the flour. Add water and scrape up any bits stuck to the bottom of the pan. When the water has almost evaporated, add stock and milk and stir until thickened, about 10 minutes, until the sauce coats the back of a spoon. If the sauce is too thick, add chicken stock to reach desired consistency.

Remove from heat; stir in chicken, peas, and herbs with salt and pepper, or to taste.

To assemble

Heat oven to 350 degrees. On a lightly floured surface, roll the dough to a circle ¼ inch thick. If using individual ramekins, cut 6 circles in the shape of the ramekins plus an extra inch around the circumference of the dishes. If using a single baking dish, cut to that shape leaving an extra inch around the sides.

Pour pot pie filling into the ramekins or baking dish. Lay pie dough over the filling and trim to ½ inch from the edge of the pan. Fold the overhang under itself to create a lip around the edge of the pan, and use your fingers to flute the edges (or use the tines of a fork to create an attractive edge). Alternatively, tuck the overhanging dough into the side of the pan. Cut 1-inch vent holes: 3–5 in a large pie or 2 in a smaller pie.

In a small bowl, lightly beat the egg with 1 tablespoon water. Lightly brush pie crust with beaten egg.

Bake pie until the crust is golden brown and the filling is bubbly, about 60 minutes for large pies, 45–50 minutes for smaller pies, and 35–40 minutes for individual ramekins.

Quick Cast Iron Skillet Chicken Pot Pie

Serves 4–6

Don't have all day to roast a chicken? This recipe was given to me by Myles Jacob, who has a cabin on Lost Girl Island on Burntside Lake. It was adapted from the *New York Times* with his spin for a quick pot pie.

2 pounds bone-in, skin-on chicken thighs

kosher salt and freshly ground black pepper

2 tablespoons extra-virgin olive oil

2 small carrots, thinly sliced

1 parsnip, thinly sliced

2 ribs celery, thinly sliced

3 cloves garlic, finely chopped

1 medium onion, finely chopped

1 (8-ounce) package portobello mushrooms, sliced

1 tablespoon coarsely chopped fresh thyme leaves

⅓ cup all-purpose flour

3 cups chicken broth

1 cup frozen peas

¼ cup finely chopped parsley

1 sheet frozen puff pastry (from a 17.3-ounce package), thawed

1 large egg

Heat oven to 425 degrees. Season chicken with salt and pepper. Heat oil in a 10-inch cast iron skillet (or other heavy-bottomed, ovenproof skillet) over medium heat. Sear chicken, skin-side down, until deeply golden brown, 6 minutes. Flip chicken and continue to cook on all sides until evenly browned and cooked through, an additional 8–10 minutes. Remove chicken and set aside to cool.

To the skillet drippings, add carrots, parsnip, celery, garlic, onions, mushrooms, and thyme. Season with salt and pepper and cook, stirring occasionally, until vegetables are tender and just cooked through, about 6 minutes. Add flour and stir to coat all the vegetables. Cook, stirring constantly, until the flour has started to turn a light golden brown with no white bits left, about 3 minutes. Add the broth ½ cup at a time, using a wooden spoon to blend and scraping up any browned bits on the bottom of the skillet. Once all the broth is added, bring to a simmer and remove from heat.

Remove the bones and skin from the cooked chicken and shred the meat into bite-size pieces. (The chicken will cook longer in the oven, so don't worry if there are pink parts remaining.) Add the chicken, peas, and parsley to the skillet, stirring to combine, and season once more with salt and pepper to taste.

Carefully unfold the puff pastry and roll it into a 12-inch circle. Place it on top of the skillet, letting some of the dough hang off the sides.

Whisk the egg with 1 teaspoon of water and brush the top of the puff pastry. Cut 3 (2½-inch) slits, about 1 inch apart. Place the skillet on a baking sheet to catch drips and place in the oven. Bake until the puff pastry is golden brown and the filling is starting to bubble up, 20–25 minutes. Reduce temperature to 375 degrees and continue to cook until puff pastry is baked through and filling has thickened considerably, another 15–20 minutes. Remove from heat and let cool 10 minutes before eating.

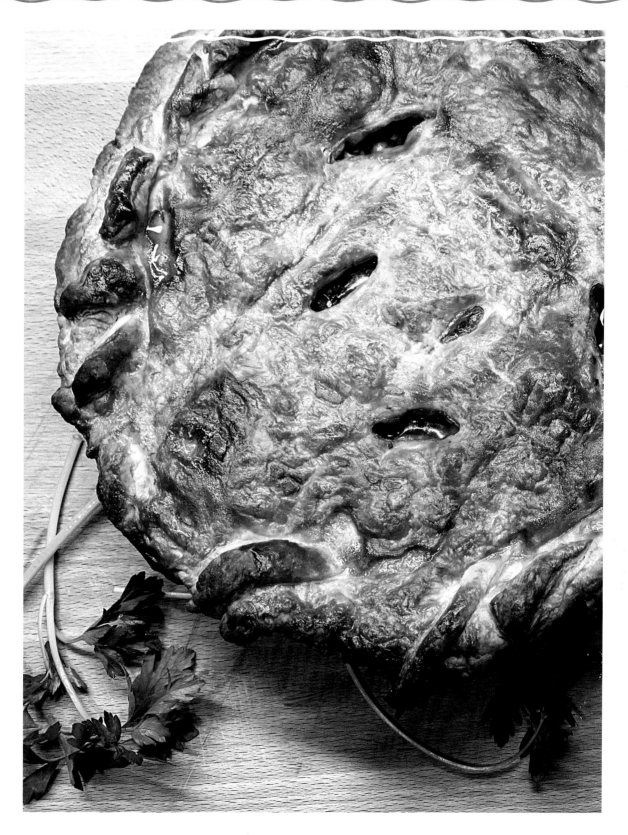

Caramelized Onion Balsamic Pasta

Serves 4

Onions, like potatoes, are a staple we always keep on hand at the island. If we find ourselves with too many onions or with onions that are starting to get old or squishy, we often caramelize them. You can store caramelized onions in ice cube trays and freeze them for use on sandwiches or pizza. I like making caramelized onions so we can have this pasta dish, which is wonderful as a main course or served alongside roasted chicken or a grilled steak.

2 tablespoons extra-virgin olive oil

2 tablespoons unsalted butter, plus more as needed

3 large yellow onions, thinly sliced

3 medium cloves garlic, minced or grated

½ teaspoon crushed red pepper

1½ teaspoons kosher salt

2 tablespoons quality balsamic vinegar

12 ounces linguine, spaghetti, or other long pasta

¾ cup finely grated Parmesan cheese, divided

¼ cup finely chopped parsley

freshly ground black pepper

Heat oil and butter in a large, heavy pot or Dutch oven over medium heat. Add onions and cook, stirring occasionally, until deeply golden brown, about 30 minutes. Add garlic and stir for 1 minute. Add crushed red pepper and salt. Stir in balsamic vinegar. Remove pot from heat.

Meanwhile, cook pasta in a large pot of boiling water, stirring occasionally, until al dente. Drain, reserving ½ cup pasta cooking liquid.

Add pasta and reserved cooking liquid to onion mixture and stir to combine (sauce should be glossy and shiny). Add a tablespoon of butter if mixture seems dry. Add ½ cup grated Parmesan cheese and stir until melted. Stir in parsley.

Divide pasta among bowls. Top with remaining ¼ cup grated Parmesan cheese. Finish with black pepper to taste.

Tomahawk Steak

**Serves 2 generously or
4 with lots of side dishes**

The tomahawk steak seems to be all the rage these days. It's big and impressive on the grill, and one steak can feed up to four people. We first cooked a tomahawk on an open flame at the point of True North Island. Keep in mind that a steak this big cooks more like a roast than a steak, so slow cooking is key to get the internal temperature just right. Try that on an open flame! That first time, the outside was crispy and almost black, but the inside was a nice medium-rare pink — it ate just fine — but the second time we opted for the grill so we could control the indirect heat and temperature. For serving, I like to cut the steak away from the bone first, then slice it into half-inch strips. Zup's grocery store usually keeps a few tomahawks on hand.

For steak rub
2 teaspoons kosher salt

2 teaspoons brown sugar

1 teaspoon black pepper

½ teaspoon ground turmeric

½ teaspoon paprika

½ teaspoon chili powder

¼ teaspoon garlic powder

¼ teaspoon onion powder

1 (30- to 40-ounce) tomahawk steak

Combine steak rub ingredients. Remove the steak from its packaging and pat dry. Generously season both sides of the steak with the rub. Allow the steak to sit at room temperature for 1 hour after seasoning.

Meanwhile, heat grill until the temperature reaches 475–525 degrees. Before grilling, wrap the entire exposed bone in foil to prevent it from burning. Sear both sides of the steak for 2 minutes per side until you get beautiful grill marks. Move the steak to the cooler side of the grill (about 300 degrees). Grill on indirect heat for approximately 30 minutes, flipping every 10 minutes, until internal temperature reaches 130 degrees for medium-rare.

Let the steak rest for 10 to 15 minutes while the internal temperature settles another 10 degrees higher. Then slice, serve, and enjoy.

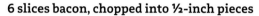

Drunken Cowboy Beans

Serves 8-10 as a side dish

My husband, Kurt, has a thing about grilled steak and beans. I must admit that the complexity of beans cooked with onions, peppers, and garlic can be a much better accompaniment than mashed, steamed, or fried potatoes. It could also be that Kurt has a fantasy of sitting around the campfire after a long day in the saddle rounding up them doggies and eating steak and beans while sipping a Corona with lime. Hence, Drunken Cowboy Beans.

6 slices bacon, chopped into ½-inch pieces

1 cup finely chopped onion

1 cup finely chopped green or red bell pepper

3 cloves garlic, minced

¼ cup finely chopped cilantro stems

1 pound dried pinto beans, rinsed and soaked in cold water overnight, then drained

1 (10-ounce) can diced tomatoes with green chilies (RO*TEL Original)

12 ounces Mexican beer (Corona)

2 cups chicken or vegetable stock

2 teaspoons kosher salt

1 teaspoon cumin

1 teaspoon black pepper

chopped cilantro leaves, for serving

In a large pot over medium heat, cook bacon for 3 minutes, stirring often. Add onions and peppers and cook, stirring, for 3 minutes more. Add garlic and cilantro stems and cook, stirring, for 30 seconds. Add drained beans, tomatoes, beer, stock, salt, cumin, and pepper, and mix well. Bring to a boil, then lower the heat to simmer for 45 minutes. Cook until soft; some beans take longer than others, so sample for chewiness. Season to taste. The beans will thicken as they cool. Serve with chopped cilantro as a garnish.

Parmesan-Stuffed Roasted Tomatoes

Serves 4

I'm crazy about steakhouse side dishes. My favorites include duck fat french fries, spinach gratin, baked potatoes, and garlicky mushrooms. These Parmesan-stuffed roasted tomatoes are a fresh take on a standard steakhouse side dish, perfect served with a thick porterhouse or ribeye.

2 medium vine-ripened tomatoes

1 teaspoon kosher salt

½ cup panko bread crumbs (or substitute crushed saltine crackers)

1 clove garlic, minced or grated

2 tablespoons finely chopped fresh thyme leaves

1 tablespoon finely chopped parsley

freshly ground black pepper

½ cup grated Parmesan cheese, divided

¼ cup extra-virgin olive oil, plus more for drizzling

Heat oven to 400 degrees. Slice tomatoes in half horizontally. Scoop out pulp and seeds, leaving about ¼ inch of flesh all the way around. Chop pulp and seeds; set aside. Season the tomatoes with salt and turn upside down in the sink or on a rack to drain additional liquid from the pulp. Place the tomatoes in a baking dish or pan that will fit them snugly.

Mix reserved pulp and seeds with bread crumbs, garlic, thyme, parsley, black pepper, ¼ cup Parmesan cheese, and olive oil. Fill tomatoes with bread crumb mixture, sprinkle with remaining ¼ cup Parmesan cheese, and drizzle the tops with olive oil. Bake until tomatoes are cooked through and tops are golden brown, about 20 minutes.

Rosemary Lemon Grilled Lamb Chops

Serves 4

Why is lamb the polarizing protein? It's one of the more tender meats available, made even more delectable when marinated in garlic, olive oil, lemon juice, and herbs. Over the years I've introduced many people to lamb on Burntside Lake, and now they cook it themselves and order it at restaurants. Grilled lamb chops are the gateway to loving lamb. Give this a try if you've never indulged.

2 large cloves garlic, crushed

2 teaspoons lemon zest

2 teaspoons fresh rosemary leaves, plus sprigs for garnish

1 teaspoon fresh thyme leaves

1 teaspoon kosher salt

3 tablespoons extra-virgin olive oil, plus more for brushing

6 lamb chops, about ¾ inch thick

2 lemons, cut in half vertically

To the bowl of a food processor add the garlic, lemon zest, rosemary, thyme, and salt. Pulse until combined. Pour in olive oil and pulse into a paste. Massage the paste into both sides of the lamb chops and let them marinate in the refrigerator for at least 2 hours (or overnight).

Bring lamb chops to room temperature, which will take about 45 minutes to an hour. Meanwhile, brush the cut side of the lemon halves with olive oil.

Heat grill to 400 degrees, add the lemon halves cut side down, and char for 4–5 minutes. Add the lamb chops and sear for about 2 minutes. Flip chops and cook for another 3 minutes for medium rare (internal temperature 125–130 degrees).

Serve chops and grilled lemons on a platter with rosemary sprigs as a garnish.

Grilled Green Onions

Serves 2

This very simple and easy side dish looks rustic on a platter of grilled meats.

8 green onions, root ends trimmed

1 tablespoon extra-virgin olive oil

kosher salt

freshly ground black pepper

1 lemon

Toss green onions with olive oil, salt, and pepper. Grill green onions, turning once, until well charred and tender, about 1 minute per side. Transfer green onions to a platter and use a microplane grater to zest some lemon peel over the green onions. Top with a squeeze of lemon juice.

Roasted Chicken with Thyme and Lemon

Serves 4-6

There are certain dishes that everyone who even remotely considers themselves a decent cook needs to master. These are everyday or every week dishes that require a certain finesse: mashed potatoes, steamed vegetables, and grilled chicken breasts don't count. Grilling or frying a steak to the perfect temperature is one. Another is simple white rice (I am still working on this one). And then there's a whole roasted chicken. They're inexpensive, they hold tons of flavor — not only from the skin and fat but also from the herbs you use — and they look impressive on a platter. This recipe has an initial cooking time of thirty minutes at a high temperature, and then the bird is roasted low and slow for two hours. I think it's hard to overcook a chicken (and a sin to have pink meat in the thigh joints), so I like to see the skin a darker brown and pulling away from the knuckle end of the drumstick. There are a million ways to jazz up roasted chicken with different flavor profiles and combinations. Try substituting rosemary or sage for the thyme. Use lime or orange juice in place of the lemons and zest. Use sesame oil with Chinese five spice instead of the butter rub, or glaze the chicken with maple syrup or Dijon mustard prior to roasting.

1 lemon, zested and sliced in half, plus additional wedges for serving

4 tablespoons unsalted butter, softened

6 cloves garlic, minced

8 sprigs fresh thyme, divided

1 (3½- to 4½-pound) whole organic chicken

kosher salt

freshly ground black pepper

Heat oven to 425 degrees. Mix lemon zest with softened butter, garlic, and thyme leaves from 4 sprigs of thyme. Dry the chicken with a paper towel. Loosen the chicken skin above the breast and around the legs and rub half the butter underneath the skin. Rub the rest of the butter on the outside of the chicken. Season inside and out with salt and pepper. Place the remaining 4 sprigs of thyme and the lemon halves inside the chicken cavity.

Place the prepared chicken in a roasting pan or large cast iron skillet. Roast chicken for 30 minutes. Reduce heat to 350 degrees and roast for 1 more hour, until chicken is nicely browned and the skin is crisp and golden. To check for doneness, poke a knife into the leg joints and pierce the meat. If juices run clear, the chicken is done. If you see a rosy-pink color, it needs more time. Continue to roast, checking every 5 minutes, until juices run clear. Carve chicken and serve with lemon wedges.

Maple Baked Beans

Serves 10 as a side dish

I make these beans no fewer than three times each summer as a side dish for barbecued ribs or chicken, roasted pork shoulder, or brats. The recipe is easy and, if you feel fancy, you can weave the bacon strips on top of the beans.

2 (16-ounce) cans baked beans

¼ cup honey

¼ cup maple syrup

¼ cup brown sugar

1 cup finely chopped onion

½ cup dried cranberries

6 strips bacon

Heat oven to 350 degrees. In a 2.5-quart Dutch oven, combine beans, honey, maple syrup, brown sugar, onions, and cranberries. Top with bacon strips. Bake until the bacon is deep brown and crisp, about 45 minutes to 1 hour. Let stand for 15 minutes before serving.

Glazed Ginger Chicken Thighs

Serves 4

Chicken thighs are the least expensive cut of meat on the market. You can buy them bone-in (best for grilling) or boneless. If you're serving a lot of folks, this recipe is a good one to double or triple for a crowd. Serve the chicken thighs over a bed of Ginger-Cilantro Rice (page 37) on a beautiful platter. Garnish with chopped cilantro.

½ cup thinly sliced green onions

3 tablespoons soy sauce

2 tablespoons dark brown sugar

1 tablespoon honey

1 tablespoon sesame oil

1 tablespoon minced or grated garlic

2 teaspoons toasted sesame seeds

1 teaspoon grated fresh ginger (no need to peel)

1 teaspoon chili paste (like sambal oelek)

8 bone-in, skin-on chicken thighs

Combine green onions, soy sauce, brown sugar, honey, sesame oil, garlic, sesame seeds, ginger, and chili paste in a bowl. Reserve ¼ cup of the mixture. Pour remaining mixture in a zip-top bag and add chicken. Marinate for a minimum of 1 hour and up to overnight.

Grill chicken at 375–400 degrees for 10 to 13 minutes, until internal temperature reaches 165 degrees. Transfer chicken to a platter and drizzle with reserved soy sauce mixture.

Ginger-Cilantro Rice

Serves 4 as a side dish

1 cup long-grain white rice

1 (inch-long) piece fresh ginger, cut into 6 rounds, plus 1 tablespoon grated fresh ginger (no need to peel; see tip)

1⅔ cups chicken broth

1 teaspoon kosher salt

1 cup chopped cilantro

2 green onions, thinly sliced, plus 1 tablespoon sliced green tops, for garnish

2 tablespoons extra-virgin olive oil

1 tablespoon toasted sesame oil

2 teaspoons unseasoned rice vinegar

black pepper

Combine rice and ginger rounds in a large saucepan. Add broth and salt. Bring to a boil, stirring often. Cover, reduce heat to low, and simmer until rice is tender and broth is absorbed, about 20 minutes.

Meanwhile, combine cilantro, green onions, and grated ginger using a food processor or blender. Add olive oil, sesame oil, and unseasoned rice vinegar. Blend until almost smooth. Season to taste with salt and freshly cracked black pepper.

Transfer rice to a bowl. Mix in cilantro-oil dressing. Serve with reserved sliced green onions as garnish.

TIP: Freeze the ginger for 30 minutes to make it easier to grate.

Grilled Leg of Lamb with Mustard Crust

Serves 4-6

Memorial Day is the "official" opening of True North Island. Also, it often lands on my birthday weekend, and we usually have a crew of people over for a dinner party. It's our annual tradition to welcome Memorial Day guests with grilled leg of lamb.

1 (4- to 5-pound) boneless leg of lamb (see tip)

For marinade
3 cloves garlic, chopped

¼ cup extra-virgin olive oil

1 tablespoon finely chopped fresh rosemary leaves

1 tablespoon finely chopped fresh thyme leaves

zest from 1 lemon

For mustard crust
3 medium cloves garlic

½ cup extra-virgin olive oil

½ cup whole-grain Dijon mustard

¼ cup fresh lemon juice

1 tablespoon finely chopped fresh rosemary leaves

1 tablespoon finely chopped fresh thyme leaves

For marinade
Combine the marinade ingredients in a bowl. Place lamb in a large shallow container and massage the ingredients into both sides of the flesh. Cover and let sit in the refrigerator for a minimum of 3 hours and up to overnight.

For mustard crust
Take lamb out of the refrigerator.

In the bowl of a food processor or blender, combine mustard crust ingredients and blend until a coarse puree forms. Spread mixture all over the lamb. Cover and let sit on the kitchen counter for 2 hours before grilling. The lamb should be close to room temperature.

To grill lamb
Cook the prepared lamb over high heat until well seared, 8–10 minutes. Flip and continue to cook 8–10 minutes more, until the second side is seared and the meat registers 130 degrees on an instant-read thermometer inserted into the thickest part of the lamb. Transfer to a cutting board, tent with foil, and let rest for 15 minutes. Slice and serve.

TIP: Buy the lamb deboned from the butcher, or purchase it held together in a net in a roast shape at the grocery store. Cut any fat cap off the roast and lay out roast with the inside meat exposed. Make small cuts in the larger pieces of meat (butterfly) for a uniform 2-inch thickness.

Gourmet Club Olive and Turmeric Couscous

Serves 8

Gourmet clubs were all the rage back in the nineties, and we belonged to one with five other young couples. We'd get together four times a year, rotating houses and hosts. The host would choose a menu and assign each couple a recipe to cook and bring to the party. The dinner parties were always fun, with plenty of cocktails and wine and foods that may not have been part of our regular recipe repertoire. This couscous dish was born from one of those parties and is a great side dish for lamb or chicken. Over time, with the growth of our individual families and careers, three of the couples moved out to the suburbs, and the gourmet club fad had run its course. This dish and the poppy seed cake that follows are two of the few recipes that outlasted the club and are island family favorites.

½ cup (1 stick) butter

6 cups chopped onion

1 teaspoon ground ginger

1 teaspoon ground turmeric

2¼ cups chicken stock

1 cup kalamata olives, pitted and sliced

¼ cup fresh lemon juice

2 cups couscous

½ cup chopped fresh basil

⅓ cup chopped fresh mint

kosher salt

freshly ground black pepper

In a medium saucepan, melt the butter over medium heat. Add onions and cook until translucent, about 20 minutes. Stir in ginger and turmeric. Add stock, olives, lemon juice, and couscous. Bring to a simmer and stir for 1 minute. Cover the pot and remove from heat. Let sit for 12 minutes while couscous cooks through. Fluff couscous with a fork, then stir in basil and mint. Season with salt and pepper. This dish can be served at room temperature or cold — straight from the refrigerator.

Poppy Seed Cake

Serves 10-12

This recipe is a favorite among my friends, and it's perfect for baby showers, weddings, birthday parties, and pretty much any celebration that calls for cake. Feel free to use a boxed white cake mix as a shortcut (we're in the no-snob zone here). I typically make this cake in a 9x13–inch pan, but I've also used two 8-inch rounds, spreading the custard filling between the two layers and frosting the top and sides with whipped cream before refrigerating to set.

For cake
¼ cup poppy seeds

2 cups 2 percent milk, divided

1 teaspoon almond extract

1 teaspoon vanilla extract

¼ cup vegetable oil

3 cups plus 2 tablespoons all-purpose flour

2½ teaspoons baking powder

½ teaspoon kosher salt

1 cup (2 sticks) unsalted butter, at room temperature

1¾ cups granulated sugar

6 large egg whites, at room temperature

For custard
1 (12-ounce) can evaporated milk

½ teaspoon kosher salt

3 large egg yolks, lightly beaten

2 tablespoons cornstarch

⅔ cup granulated sugar

1 teaspoon vanilla extract

½ cup (1 stick) butter, cut into small pieces

For whipped frosting
1 (8-ounce) carton heavy cream

2 teaspoons confectioners' sugar

1 teaspoon vanilla extract

¼ teaspoon cream of tartar

For cake
Heat oven to 350 degrees. Prepare a 9x13–inch pan with cooking spray or butter and flour. Soak the poppy seeds in ¾ cup milk for 5 minutes. Strain seeds; discard milk.

In a medium bowl, combine almond extract, vanilla extract, remaining 1¼ cups milk, and oil; set aside. In a large bowl, combine flour, baking powder, and salt; set aside.

Place butter in a stand mixer with a paddle attachment and beat until smooth. Sprinkle in granulated sugar and whip on high for 5 minutes. Add egg whites, 1 at a time, to the butter mixture while mixing on low speed, letting fully combine after each addition. Add in one-third of the dry ingredients to the egg-butter mixture and mix on low speed until just combined. Add in one-half of the liquid ingredients, then one-third of the dry, then remaining liquid, then remaining dry, mixing after each addition. Add poppy seeds and mix until just combined.

Pour the batter into the prepared cake pan and bake for 25 to 30 minutes, until a toothpick poked in the center comes out clean. Cool cake on a rack.

For custard

Whisk evaporated milk, salt, egg yolks, cornstarch, granulated sugar, and vanilla in a pot. Add butter pieces to the pot. Cook on medium-high heat, whisking constantly, until mixture comes to a boil and thickens, about 3–4 minutes. (It will burn easily, so keep a close watch.) Set aside to cool.

For whipped frosting

Pour cream, confectioners' sugar, vanilla, and cream of tartar into a cold mixing bowl and whisk on high speed until medium-stiff peaks form, about 1 minute.

To assemble

Pour cooled custard onto the cake and spread to the edges. Frost the cake with the whipped cream, being careful to keep the layers separate. Refrigerate until serving.

Rhubarb Custard Pie

Serves 8

This recipe was adapted from one handed down by my husband Kurt's grandmother, Edna DeBower. Edna grew up on a farm in Nebraska along the Platte River. Back then they called dinner *supper* and lunch *dinner*, and often the big meal of the day was served at noon, with leftovers for supper. At seed planting time, Edna and her sisters (and other close relatives there to help) prepared huge dinners for the hired hands. Rhubarb pie was the highlight of these early summer dinners, and Edna was renowned for her crust. Rhubarb, its red stalks picked around Memorial Day, is the first pie of the season. Back then, Edna used lard in her pies, the best lard — leaf lard — coming from the leaf-shaped chunk of fat that surrounds a pig's kidneys. I prefer high-fat butter such as Kerrygold if you can find it; otherwise, any unsalted butter will do. Of course, the highlight of harvesttime was apple pie, but that's another recipe.

For crust

1¼ cups all-purpose flour

1 teaspoon kosher salt

1 cup (2 sticks) high-fat, unsalted butter (such as Kerrygold), chilled and cut into ½-inch cubes

3 tablespoons ice water

1 tablespoon vodka

For filling

1 pound rhubarb (about 4 large stalks or 8 small stalks), cut into ½-inch pieces (4 cups)

1 cup granulated sugar, divided

1 teaspoon orange zest

3 large eggs

⅓ cup heavy cream

¼ cup all-purpose flour

1 teaspoon ground cinnamon

½ teaspoon kosher salt

For crust

In bowl of a food processor, pulse flour and salt 2 to 3 times, until combined. Scatter cubed butter over flour and pulse 4 to 5 times, until flour is evenly distributed. (Dough should look crumbly.) Add 3 tablespoons ice water through the food processor tube, pulsing once after each addition. The crumbs should begin to form larger clusters. Add the vodka and continue to pulse until the dough comes together in a ball and awkwardly spins in the machine.

Remove dough from bowl and place in a mound on a clean surface. Work the dough just enough to form a ball. Cut the ball in half, then form each half into a disk. Wrap each disk with plastic wrap and refrigerate for at least 1 hour.

Roll out 1 dough disk into a 9-inch circle. Place into a pie plate, then push the dough up the sides to form an edge. (Save second disk for another pie.)

For filling

Heat oven to 400 degrees. Place a baking sheet on the middle oven rack. In a bowl, stir together rhubarb with ¼ cup sugar and orange zest. Transfer the rhubarb mixture to the crust in an even layer.

In a mixing bowl, combine eggs with the cream and whisk until smooth. Stir in the flour, cinnamon, salt, and remaining ¾ cup sugar, then pour over the rhubarb mixture.

Bake for approximately 15 minutes, then reduce heat to 375 degrees to bake for another 30 minutes, until the pie crust is lightly browned and the center is set and no longer wet in the middle. Cool completely before serving.

Cast Iron Rhubarb Skillet Cake

Serves 8

This recipe is adapted from rhubarb spoon cake in *The Lost Kitchen*, a memoir by Erin French. I instantly fell in love with the recipe and knew it would be great to make with the discarded solids or "rough jam" after finishing a batch of Rhubarb Syrup (see page 11). I also knew it would be a rock-solid cabin recipe if I could bake the cake in a cast iron skillet. This cake can be served as a brunch item or for dessert with ice cream or whipped cream.

For jam (see tip)

3 cups rhubarb chopped into ½-inch pieces

¼ cup granulated sugar

1 teaspoon lemon zest

2 teaspoons fresh lemon juice

2 teaspoons cornstarch

For cake

1 cup all-purpose flour, plus more for the pan

2 teaspoons baking powder

½ cup granulated sugar

¼ cup brown sugar

1 teaspoon kosher salt

½ teaspoon ground ginger

1 large egg

1 teaspoon vanilla extract

½ cup 2 percent milk

¼ cup sour cream

½ cup (1 stick) unsalted butter, melted and cooled, plus more for the pan

For jam

In a medium saucepan, combine the rhubarb, sugar, lemon zest, lemon juice, and cornstarch. Bring to a simmer over medium heat, stirring constantly, until the rhubarb is tender and sauce-like, about 10 minutes. Remove from heat and allow to cool to room temperature.

For cake

Heat oven to 400 degrees. Coat a 10-inch cast iron skillet with butter and dust with flour, shaking out any excess flour. In a medium bowl, whisk together flour, baking powder, granulated sugar, brown sugar, salt, and ginger. In a large bowl, whisk together the egg, vanilla, milk, sour cream, and cooled, melted butter. Gently stir the wet ingredients into the dry until just incorporated.

Pour about two-thirds of the batter into the prepared cast iron skillet and spread evenly. Plop the rhubarb rough jam by the tablespoonful in 4 to 5 areas of the cake. Pour the remaining cake batter over top, then dollop on the remaining rough jam by the tablespoonful. Use a small knife to swirl together the batter and jam and smooth out the top.

Bake until a toothpick inserted in the middle of the cake comes out clean, about 25 minutes. Serve the cake directly from the skillet.

TIP: You can also use the solids from the Rhubarb Syrup recipe, page 11.

Easy Rhubarb Custard Bars

Serves 8

Minnesota is the home of bar cookies, and these rhubarb custard bars would be at home on any potluck table.

2½ cups all-purpose flour, divided

¾ cup confectioners' sugar

1 cup (2 sticks) unsalted butter, softened

1 teaspoon vanilla extract

4 large eggs

2 cups granulated sugar

1½ teaspoons kosher salt

4 cups rhubarb chopped into ¼- to ½-inch pieces

Heat oven to 350 degrees. Grease a 9x13–inch pan with butter or shortening. In a bowl, mix together 2 cups flour, confectioners' sugar, softened butter, and vanilla. Press crust into prepared pan. Bake for 15 minutes and remove from the oven.

While the crust is baking, in a large bowl use a wooden spoon to stir together eggs, sugar, remaining ½ cup flour, and salt until well combined; stir in the rhubarb. Spoon the rhubarb mixture onto the crust. Bake for 45 minutes. Let cool for at least 15 minutes before cutting into squares.

Laura's Favorite Cookies

Makes about 24 cookies

These were cookies Grandma Bea made for my sister, Laura, when we'd come to visit each summer in Waupaca, Wisconsin. My sister died in a car accident in 1979, and for many years these cookies disappeared from my grandmother's house. Fast-forward to a conversation I had with my aunt Karen when she came to Burntside Lake recently. She'd found the recipe for "Laura's Cookies" in Grandma Bea's recipe box. The recipe card had the ingredients but none of the instructions on how to cook them. With some trial and error we figured it out. The texture of these cookies is super delicate, almost like sand, so plan accordingly if you're transporting them — if they last that long.

1 cup (2 sticks) unsalted butter, at room temperature

1 cup confectioners' sugar

1 large egg, beaten

1 teaspoon vanilla extract

2 cups all-purpose flour

½ teaspoon kosher salt

1 teaspoon baking soda

1 teaspoon cream of tartar

¼ cup finely chopped pecans

¼ cup granulated sugar

Heat oven to 400 degrees. In a stand mixer with a paddle attachment, mix together the butter and confectioners' sugar. Add the beaten egg and vanilla and mix until combined. In a large bowl, stir together flour, salt, baking soda, cream of tartar, and pecans. Mix the dry ingredients into the wet ingredients.

Roll dough into walnut-size balls (or use a cookie scoop), and place 8 balls on a parchment-lined baking sheet (this dough spreads a lot). Pour granulated sugar on a plate. Dip the bottom of a glass into warm water and then into the dish of sugar. Use the sugar-coated glass to flatten the balls, recoating glass as needed. Bake 6–8 minutes, until very light brown.

HOW THE ISLAND GOT ITS NAME

On July 4, 1999, the Boundary Waters blowdown hit True North Island. That morning I was with Kurt and Ellie, who was eleven months old. We'd been at the cabin for a few days, and the weather was perfect, with temperatures in the eighties, nearly clear skies, and cool evenings. Even that morning there were no clouds and the wind was calm. Our plan was to attend the Fourth of July parade in Ely, Ellie's first time. We'd been going to the parade for years, and it is special. The whole town comes out early, and everyone reserves their spot by setting folding chairs on the curbs lining the parade route. Starting at noon, the town police and color guard leads the way, followed by a long line of floats with people from town: the kids from the dance studio, political groups, local businesses, the fire department, and much more. The Ely High School marching band performs (I think I remember "25 or 6 to 4" by Chicago), and the Ely Klown Band, founded by veterans after World War II, plays polka favorites. Over the years we've seen the Shriners with their iconic red fezzes doing tricks on Harley-Davidson motorcycles, Cushman minibikes, and go-karts. We were all set to get in the boat and head to the mainland when we heard over WELY End of the Road Radio that a major storm cell was headed toward us and the parade and Fourth of July activities had been postponed.

Severe storms are a fact of life up on the island. In June and July, they come roaring from the southwest when pulled up by hot, moist Canadian air. In 1976 a tornado swept through the lake. It touched down on Brownell Island west of us, taking out a huge swath of trees, then jumped over True North Island and took out another swath on Miller Island directly south. Keep in mind, our island is covered with red and white pines growing on hard bedrock, and the cabin sits on timber stilts without a foundation of any sort. There's no storm shelter or cast iron tub to hide in. Once we asked a local what to do if a tornado hit us, and his response was, "Sometimes it's just your turn to die." So, when we heard the storm was coming our way, the only thing to do was double-tie the boats to the dock and close the windows facing southwest. I sat in the living room listening to WELY, holding Ellie, and watching the storm come toward us.

The storm moved in slowly. The wind was still relatively calm, but the skies turned dark gray. The hail hit us first and the screaming winds next. With the wind speed up over a hundred miles per hour, I could see the waves flatten to a rush of white foam. I was deeply scared. I scooped up Ellie and sat hunched over her in the back hallway behind the fireplace, seemingly the only safe spot, though if the house were smashed by the huge surrounding trees (we even have hundred-year-old trees growing through cut holes in our deck), we'd be smashed with it. I curled over Ellie in my lap while Kurt ran from room to room watching for God knows what. Then he said, "The sailboat is gone."

That stupid sailboat. It was a heavy, twenty-two-foot boat tied to a mooring thirty feet off the shoreline in the channel between our island and the neighbor's. I saw Kurt in the bedroom undressing and pulling on his shorty wet suit. I screamed, "What are you doing?!" He said he needed to catch the sailboat before it smashed into the rocks. How he would keep a two-thousand-pound boat off the rocks, I had no idea. And I don't think he did either. I was mad and scared and screaming, "Don't do it!" He said nothing but opened the sliding glass door to the earsplitting wind. I said something I regret now: "Go ahead, leave us to save the stupid sailboat, go get yourself killed. We'll be fine!"

About five minutes later, the storm passed. Kurt was safe — and so was the sailboat. Its cast iron keel caught on a submerged rock just off the shore, and Kurt was able to pull it away by throwing the bow anchor out into deeper water and at the same time tying the stern to a tree on shore. The sky was clear and blue almost as soon as the storm passed. Trees were down all over the island, but none hit the cabin. We were lucky: about a mile northeast of us, in the Boundary Waters Canoe Area, the storm blew down every single tree in a path a mile wide and ten miles long. Pictures of the devastation look like thousands of toothpicks lying there waiting for some giant to start a game of pick-up sticks. Now, twenty years later, all those toothpicks have become a fire hazard waiting for a spark.

But this story is about how our island got its name. For years, it didn't have an official name. We think the islanders around us called it "Trash Island" because they all used it to dump their refuse. Kurt, his brother, and their father spent the first two years after its purchase re-bagging and bringing load after load of trash to the town dump. Then, it was just informally called "Johnson Island" because that's my husband's surname. If we had a fire on the island, there was no way to give an address to find us. Two years after the blow-down, someone from St. Louis County, without our input, gave us a new name and address: 2431 Jig Island. For our family, that name did not resonate. My mother-in-law, Dolores, contacted county officials in Duluth and lobbied for a name change. After much cajoling, they agreed. She named the island True North.

And now back to the storm. It passed, the sky turned blue, and the winds completely abated. WELY radio announced that the parade was back on. We changed, jumped in the boat, motored to Burntside Lodge, which also made it through the blowdown reasonably unscathed, and rode into town to see the parade. The Shriners drove their funny go-karts in figure eights, the high school band played something like "A Hard Day's Night," the Ely Auto Club showed off their hot rods and muscle cars, Zup's supermarket employees threw out handfuls of candy, the miners picketed for more jobs, the environmentalists picketed for no more mines, the mayor waved from the back of a vintage convertible, and the Klown Band stole the show by performing the polka hymn "In Heaven There Is No Beer" while we all sang along.

The Perfect Island Bloody Mary

Serves 1

While writing this book I asked each family member what some of their signature dishes are or what recipes remind them of True North Island. My niece Brittany talked about our bloody Marys — spicy V8 with lots of Worcestershire sauce and Herdez Salsa Verde, which we think first made its way to the island when my mother-in-law, Dolores, vacationed there while working in Texas at the Houston Grand Opera. For an extra-special bloody Mary, roll the juice of a lime over the rim of your glass, then dip the glass in Lawry's Seasoned Salt, kosher salt, or Tajín.

1 lemon wedge

1 lime wedge

2 ounces vodka

4 ounces spicy tomato juice (V8 Spicy Hot 100% Vegetable Juice)

1 teaspoon prepared horseradish

2 dashes hot sauce (Tabasco)

3 dashes Worcestershire sauce

dash seasoned salt (Lawry's)

1 grind freshly cracked black pepper

1 teaspoon salsa verde (Herdez)

garnishes of choice: pickle spear; green olive; pickled carrots, dilly beans, or asparagus; celery stalk; cheese cubes

Fill a collins (10- to 14-ounce) glass with ice. Squeeze the lemon and lime wedges into the glass and drop them in. Add the vodka, tomato juice, horseradish, hot sauce, Worcestershire sauce, seasoned salt, black pepper, and salsa verde and stir. Garnish as desired.

Lila's Simply Perfect Margarita

Serves 1

My mother-in-law, Dolores Johnson, and Lila Jacob were neighbors in south Minneapolis. They each had three children and started their married lives as stay-at-home moms with busy, career-minded husbands. Dolores's husband was in advertising; Lila's was a doctor. The families lived on the same block, and their children became fast friends, running wild through the neighborhood playing kick the can and abandoning their bikes in one another's yards when it was time for dinner. When Dolores's son, Kurt, was in sixth grade, both moms decided to send their boys to summer camp. Camp Easton was located on Little Long Lake, one portage from Burntside Lake. When it came time for Parents' Weekend, both families stayed at Burntside Lodge. It was on this trip that the parents fell in love with Ely and Burntside Lake, and eventually they bought adjoining lots on Lost Girl Island. The lots were undeveloped, and the families made a tent village at the water's edge. After two summers and a particularly wet spring, Kurt's parents bought the nearby True North Island. The families have remained lifelong friends. The Jacobs and the Johnsons have spent many summer nights with dinner parties and cocktails out on our deck. Early on, Ellie was dubbed an honorary Jacob boy due to her raspy, loud voice and propensity for staying dirty from sunup to sundown. At those dinner parties, Lila would break out her famous simply perfect margaritas.

2 ounces silver tequila

2 ounces Cointreau or simple syrup

2 ounces fresh lime juice

lime wedges

kosher salt

Fill a cocktail shaker with ice and add the tequila, orange liqueur or simple syrup, and lime juice. Shake to combine all ingredients. Run the edge of a lime wedge around a rocks glass. Dip the edge of the glass in a small pile of kosher salt. Add ice to the glass. Strain the contents of the shaker into the ice-filled glass. Garnish with a fresh lime wedge.

Juneberry Drink Syrup

When Ellie moved to college, we sold her childhood house and downsized to a townhome in St. Paul. Our idea was that we would spend more time on True North Island in the summer and travel in the winter. Our first spring in the townhome I noticed all the trees grew red berries that later turned deep purple. The birds ate these berries like crazy. My neighbor said they were serviceberry trees and the berries, affectionately known as Juneberries, could be eaten. Through research I found recipes to make syrup from the berries to use in drinks, in cocktail shrubs, or on pancakes. My neighbors watched curiously as I picked all the berries on the property, and over the next week I made cruets of syrup that I brought to each of them. To my surprise, I noticed serviceberry trees on the mainland in Ely, and now each spring I make Juneberry syrup. This syrup can be replicated with blackberries, blueberries, or raspberries. Adjust the sugar as needed based on the sweetness of the berries you pick.

3 cups fresh Juneberries, rinsed, stems removed

1 cup water

⅓ cup granulated sugar

2 tablespoons fresh lemon juice

In a medium heavy-duty saucepan, combine berries with water and sugar. Bring to a boil over medium-high heat, reduce the heat to medium-low, and simmer until the berries are very soft and juicy, about 5 minutes.

Set a fine mesh sieve over a bowl. Pour the berry pulp into the sieve and allow the juice to drip through. Gently press the pulp with a rubber spatula to extract as much juice as possible. Stir in lemon juice. Transfer to a Mason jar or cruet.

Juneberry Martini Cocktail

Serves 1

1.5 ounces Juneberry Drink Syrup (page 54)

1 ounce vodka

1 ounce orange liqueur (Grand Marnier or Cointreau)

lemon twist, for garnish

Fill a cocktail shaker with ice. Add the syrup, vodka, and orange liqueur and shake to combine. Strain into a martini glass. Garnish with a twist of lemon.

Juneberry Margarita

Serves 1

lime wedge

superfine or granulated sugar, for rim

2 ounces Juneberry Drink Syrup (page 54)

3 ounces tequila

1 ounce fresh lime juice

fresh herb sprigs like cilantro or mint, for garnish

Rub the rim of a rocks or margarita glass with a lime wedge. Swirl the rim through a small pile of superfine or granulated sugar. Add ice cubes to the glass. Add the Juneberry syrup, then the tequila, and then the lime juice. Stir to combine. Squeeze lime wedge into the drink. Garnish with a fresh herb sprig.

Juneberry Burntside Tequila Sunrise

Serves 1

3 tablespoons Juneberry Drink Syrup (page 54)

2 ounces tequila

4 ounces orange juice

orange slice, for garnish

Fill a highball glass with ice. Add Juneberry syrup. In a cocktail shaker, mix tequila and orange juice. Pour slowly into glass to keep the syrup layer on the bottom, creating the layered sunrise effect. Garnish with an orange slice and serve with a straw or a long-handled spoon for mixing.

Dutch Baby Pancake

Serves 4

The puffed-up, skillet-baked Dutch baby pancake looks fabulous just out of the oven, and you can slide it onto a pretty platter or serve it right from the cast iron skillet. Make sure you use a thick oven mitt to transport the smoking-hot skillet to a trivet to avoid burning a hole in your table. To make it extra special, serve with fresh berries and confectioners' sugar or caramelized apples or bananas with brown sugar.

½ cup all-purpose flour

3 tablespoons granulated sugar

½ teaspoon kosher salt

¼ teaspoon ground cinnamon

2 large eggs, at room temperature

½ cup whole milk, at room temperature

1 teaspoon vanilla extract

3 tablespoons unsalted butter

confectioners' sugar, lemon zest, fresh fruit, honey, syrup, whipped cream, for serving, optional

Heat oven to 400 degrees. Place a 10-inch cast iron skillet in the oven for 10 minutes.

Meanwhile, in a bowl, whisk together flour, sugar, salt, and cinnamon. In a blender or a food processor (or with a whisk and a strong whisking hand), blend the eggs, milk, and vanilla until frothy, about 30 seconds. Add the dry ingredients and blend 30 seconds more, until a smooth, thin batter forms.

Pull the skillet from the oven and add the butter to let it melt, twisting to make sure the sides and the bottom are coated in butter. Pour the batter into the center of the buttered skillet and return it to the oven for 18–20 minutes, until the pancake is puffed and golden brown in some spots. (Important: do not open the oven to peek until it's done. Use your oven light if you have one.)

Pull the skillet out of the oven and slide the Dutch baby out of the pan onto a platter, or serve it straight from the skillet; just remember it will be very hot: place a trivet underneath.

If desired, sprinkle confectioners' sugar over the top, or zest a bit of lemon and add fresh fruit. Serve with honey, butter, syrup, or whipped cream. This is also delicious plain.

Dolores's Swedish Blueberry Pancakes

Serves 4

My mother-in-law, Dolores, makes the sweetest little silver dollar pancakes with fresh blueberries. This Swedish recipe has more eggs than a traditional recipe and no baking powder. The pancakes are a bit thinner than a traditional pancake, like slightly thicker crepes. Nothing is better than sitting outside on the deck, drinking strong black coffee, and eating a pile of pancakes from a tin plate.

3 large eggs

2½ cups milk

1¼ cups all-purpose flour

½ teaspoon kosher salt

3 tablespoons butter, melted

2 cups fresh blueberries

maple syrup, for serving

In a large mixing bowl, beat the eggs and milk until combined. Beat in flour and salt until smooth. Stir in melted butter.

Heat a griddle or a cast iron skillet with a small amount of vegetable oil. For each pancake, pour a scant ¼ cup batter onto the griddle, sprinkle 6–8 berries on top, and cook over medium heat, 1–2 minutes. With a spatula, turn the pancakes and cook until golden brown, about 30 seconds more.

Serve immediately with real maple syrup, or keep warm on a plate in the oven while making the remaining pancakes.

Grilled Onion and Avocado Guacamole

Makes about 2½ cups

Grilling the onions and avocados lends a smokiness to this guacamole. The first time I saw a recipe that called for grilling avocados, I thought, *Who'd be crazy enough to grill an avocado?* And then I tried it. You should too.

4 ripe avocados, sliced in half lengthwise, pits removed

2 limes, cut in half crosswise

1 small red onion, peeled and cut in half crosswise

1 jalapeño, cut in half lengthwise, seeded

extra-virgin olive oil

kosher salt

freshly cracked black pepper

¼ cup chopped cilantro

Brush cut side of avocado halves, limes, red onion, and jalapeño with olive oil. Season with salt and pepper.

Heat grill over a medium-high flame. Grill onions until charred and caramelized, about 5 minutes per side. Grill jalapeño, avocados, and limes, cut side down, until grill marks appear with a light char, about 5 minutes.

When vegetables are cool enough to handle, chop jalapeño into very small pieces and place in a large bowl. Chop the onions into ¼-inch pieces and add to the bowl. Scoop out the avocado flesh and mash to desired consistency in the bowl, incorporating the jalapeño and onions. Stir in the chopped cilantro, and squeeze the grilled limes into the bowl. Season to taste with additional salt and pepper.

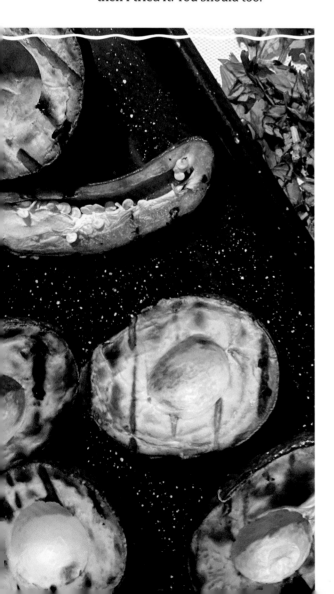

Sadie's Smoked Lake Superior Whitefish Spread

Serves 4–6

My niece Sadie grew up a little wary of my cooking. She didn't try anything remotely unfamiliar, like liver pâté or seafood ceviche. Years later, our family drove up to witness Sadie's graduation at the University of Minnesota Duluth. We had a celebratory dinner that night at the Pickwick Restaurant & Pub, and I asked if anyone would share an appetizer of smoked whitefish spread. To my surprise, Sadie said she would. Her appreciation for smoked fish was a reflection of four years in college "up north" and a new level of culinary sophistication. This recipe is dedicated to her. Now I make this dip when Sadie visits True North Island for the Hansen Family Weekend each summer.

At Zup's supermarket we can purchase smoked Lake Superior whitefish from Everett's Smoked Fish. And if we're fortunate to have a visit from our friends the McKhanns, they bring us the smoked fish from Halvorson Fisheries in Cornucopia, Wisconsin.

1 boneless smoked whitefish fillet (about 8 ounces; or substitute smoked lake trout or smoked salmon)

½ cup cream cheese, softened

¼ cup sour cream

¼ cup plain Greek yogurt

1 tablespoon prepared horseradish

1 teaspoon Dijon mustard

1 tablespoon finely chopped red onion

1 tablespoon finely chopped Italian flat-leaf parsley (or fresh dill)

juice of ½ lemon

1 tablespoon chopped green onions or finely chopped chives, for garnish

4 ribs celery cut into sticks, cucumber slices, water crackers, Triscuit crackers, or baguette, for serving

Combine whitefish, cream cheese, sour cream, yogurt, horseradish, mustard, red onion, parsley, and lemon juice in a food processor and pulse until mixed. Garnish in a pretty bowl with green onions or chives, and serve on a platter with vegetables or crackers for dipping.

Grandma Bea's Dilly Crackers

Serves 8

My grandma Bea always had a jar of these dilly crackers on her kitchen sideboard when we'd visit her each summer. Now I serve these crackers at cocktail hour on the island. When stored in a cookie jar or Mason jar, these crackers stay fresh forever — or at least for as long as they're around (they have a way of disappearing). I use Grandma Bea's original recipe, which my sister likes to call the "gourmet way." She does it the "quick way," with a packet of Hidden Valley Ranch Seasoning. Feel free to cut corners.

2 tablespoons dried dill

⅓ cup finely chopped fresh dill

¼ cup garlic powder

2 teaspoons fine sea salt

1 teaspoon black pepper

⅔ cup extra-virgin olive oil

2 (12-ounce) packages oyster crackers

Heat oven to 250 degrees. Cover 2 large baking sheets with aluminum foil.

Put dried and fresh dill, garlic powder, salt, pepper, and olive oil in a 3-quart plastic zip-top bag and shake to combine. Add oyster crackers and shake to coat. Distribute crackers evenly on prepared baking sheets. Bake for 20 minutes, shaking pans to redistribute crackers halfway through bake time. Turn off the oven, but leave the pans in for 15 more minutes so the crackers have time to lightly brown. Crackers can be kept in an airtight container for about 30 days.

Ellie's Vichyssoise

Serves 6

One of my favorite photos of Ellie shows her at about ten months old sitting in a high chair on the deck at True North Island being fed vichyssoise by Grandma Dolores, who's wearing a black T-shirt and a strand of elegant white pearls. I realize that white pearls at the cabin seems a little incongruous, but that's just my mother-in-law. She grew up on a small farm in rural Nebraska but retired as managing director of the Houston Grand Opera, one of the top five operas in the United States. Then, rather than living comfortably in Houston or Minneapolis, Dolores built a small prairie-style home back in the same small Nebraska town where she grew up. All that time, though, after her husband died young, she continued to pay the mortgage and upkeep for True North Island. When I first met Dolores, I was intimidated by her sophistication, her food knowledge, and her manners. And I guess, over time, I assimilated some of those traits. I learned to love food and cooking, I enjoyed entertaining friends with formal dinner parties, and I took on some of the traditions of entertaining on the island.

One tradition is that when island friends come over for drinks, we always set up a little bar on the cabin counter with a bowl of fresh ice. We make sure to have a cheese board or some other snack no matter what's in the cupboard: sometimes just saltines, black olives, and a handful of almonds. My shorthand for how to entertain, or for appropriate manners, or even for how to dress for a night out is WWDD — "What Would Dolores Do?" Now she lives near us in St. Paul, and we often share Sunday dinners during the fall, winter, and spring months. Come summer we're all together throughout the day on True North Island. I love spending time with Dolores, and we have grown very close. There's no one better to be with as the sun goes down over the point of the island, an extra glass of red wine in hand, having a conversation about politics, art, music, books, and especially food. And I think vichyssoise is a recipe that captures both the elegance and the down-home rural roots of my mother-in-law. It has the French sophistication, but at its core vichyssoise is simply a creamy potato soup with leeks.

4 tablespoons unsalted butter

8 leeks, white parts with a bit of
green, rinsed and sliced

3 medium Yukon Gold potatoes, cut
into small cubes

3 cups chicken broth

1½ cups heavy cream

1 teaspoon kosher salt

few grinds cracked black pepper

¼ cup chopped fresh chives,
for garnish

1 tablespoon celery leaves,
for garnish

Melt butter in a large Dutch oven over
medium-low heat. Add the leeks and
cook gently for 5 minutes. Add potatoes and chicken broth and bring to a
boil. Reduce heat to a simmer. Cook
on low heat, gently simmering for
45 minutes, until the leeks and potatoes are very soft. Remove from heat
and allow to cool for a few minutes.
Use an immersion blender to puree
the soup in the pan until smooth.
Whisk in cream, and season with salt
and pepper.

Transfer soup to a mixing bowl and
let it cool to room temperature, then
cover with plastic wrap and put into
the refrigerator to cool. Taste and
adjust seasoning; sprinkle with chives
and celery leaves for garnish. Serve
cold in chilled bowls.

Creamy Dilly Summer Salad Dressing

Makes 1 cup

When I first planted the garden at Hilltop, I grew plenty of dill for making pickles. I didn't realize then that dill is self-seeding and would come back to the garden year after year. Turns out, it's not called dill *weed* for nothing. It has spread past its borders and mixes with my onions on one side and asparagus on the other. What I also didn't know is that the dill weed looks like the asparagus plants after they've bolted in early summer, so it's somewhat of a chore to keep the two separated. Now dill makes its way into potato salads, cucumber salads, chicken salads, and anything else I can think of.

½ cup plain Greek yogurt

⅓ cup mayonnaise

2 tablespoons fresh lemon juice

1 tablespoon water

2 tablespoons finely chopped fresh dill (or 1 tablespoon dried)

1 tablespoon finely chopped parsley

1 clove garlic, minced or grated

1 teaspoon Dijon mustard

1 teaspoon kosher salt

1 teaspoon black pepper

1 teaspoon ground mustard

lemon zest, to taste

Combine all ingredients in a Mason jar. Seal the jar and shake to mix. Taste and season with additional salt and freshly cracked black pepper, as desired. Seal and shake again.

Tarragon Ranch Dressing

Makes 1 cup

Ranch dressing is an American staple up there with mac and cheese, ketchup, and Hamburger Helper. Growing up, we dumped store-bought Hidden Valley spice packets into the Hidden Valley branded glass shaker, added milk (my mother used buttermilk) and mayonnaise, and then shook vigorously. The dressing was a delicious dip that made even carrots or celery worthy of an after-school snack. Bottled Hidden Valley Ranch became a little sweeter over the years (sugar is the third ingredient after oil and water) and is just not the same, so I created my own version. I can easily make this dressing on the island with ingredients on hand.

½ cup buttermilk

¼ cup plain Greek yogurt

2 tablespoons mayonnaise

1 teaspoon dried tarragon (see tip)

1 large clove garlic, minced or grated

½ teaspoon Dijon mustard

2 teaspoons fresh lemon juice, to taste (plus some zest, optional)

2 dashes hot sauce (Tabasco)

salt, to taste

freshly cracked black pepper, to taste

Combine buttermilk, yogurt, mayonnaise, tarragon, garlic, mustard, lemon juice, and hot sauce in a Mason jar. Seal the jar, and shake to combine. Taste and season with salt and plenty of freshly cracked black pepper, as desired. Seal and shake again.

TIP: Or use 1 tablespoon fresh tarragon and add dill, parsley, chives, celery leaves, or a combination of these.

Red Cabbage Slaw

Serves 8-10

When I have family and friends on the island, I try to keep meals simple. This means lots of meats that can be tossed on the grill, easy-to-prepare starches like pasta or potatoes, and hearty salads that can be made ahead and stored for days in the refrigerator. This red cabbage slaw is perfect alongside grilled ribs or chicken, with fried fish fillets, or in fish tacos. One year when I pulled the slaw from the refrigerator for the fourth day, my nieces declared, "No more cabbage slaw!" I waited until they left and used the last of it to make a pita sandwich with some leftover grilled chicken and a dollop of plain yogurt. Slaw is so versatile.

For vinaigrette
2 teaspoons orange zest

1 cup fresh orange juice

1 teaspoon lime zest

¼ cup fresh lime juice

½ small red onion, grated

3 cloves garlic, minced or grated

1 tablespoon honey

½ cup extra-virgin olive oil

1 teaspoon kosher salt

For slaw
1 medium head red cabbage, finely sliced into ribbons

½ teaspoon kosher salt

¼ cup chopped mint leaves

¼ cup chopped Italian flat-leaf parsley

For vinaigrette
Place dressing ingredients in a small bowl and whisk until combined (or shake together in a Mason jar).

To assemble
Place cabbage in a large bowl and toss with salt to soften. Add the vinaigrette, tossing to combine, and let sit for 30 minutes in the refrigerator for the flavors to meld. Add chopped mint and parsley before serving.

NOTE: This slaw can be garnished with peanuts or slivered almonds for additional crunch.

Lemony Arugula Parmesan Salad

Serves 4

This salad is one of my favorites, and I often serve it alongside a grilled ribeye. The arugula looks beautiful spread over a platter with the sliced steak arranged on top. The two complement each other, as the lemon juice and bitterness of the arugula cut the richness of the steak. I also like this salad piled on top of a pizza fresh out of the oven (see Kurt's Pizza, page 68).

1 tablespoon fresh lemon juice

3 tablespoons extra-virgin olive oil, best quality you can find

½ teaspoon kosher salt

4 grinds freshly cracked black pepper (about ½ teaspoon), to taste

5 ounces arugula (about 4 cups)

Parmesan cheese, shaved with a vegetable peeler

In a large salad bowl, combine the lemon juice, olive oil, salt, and pepper. Place the arugula in the bowl on top of the dressing. Add shaved Parmesan cheese. Toss right before serving, and top each serving with a few more cheese ribbons.

Kurt's Pizza

Serves 8-10

The last meal on the island before we drive back to the Twin Cities is typically pizza. Pizza night is a great way to use up a leftover rib or two, dribs and drabs of cheese, vegetables left in the crisper, and sprigs of basil starting to turn brown on the windowsill. We have friends with full-blown outdoor wood-fired pizza ovens that, after a few hours of stoking, heat up to an impressive 800 degrees and cook pizzas with bubbly, charred crusts in minutes. But on the island, we're deathly afraid of fire. So we make do with our three-burner Weber gas grill and a pizza stone. To get the grill as hot as possible, cram a strip of crumpled aluminum foil along its back vent. It will take close to an hour to get the grill temperature, and most importantly the stone, up over 500 degrees. The pizza dough, rolled very thin, with toppings, will cook in five to ten minutes. Keep your toppings to a minimum and the sauce to within a half inch of the outer crust, and watch the amounts of cheese—no need to be the cheese queen of the north. We cook anywhere from four to six pizzas on pizza night, setting each aside until they're all done. Right before serving, we slide each pie back onto the stone for a quick reheat.

For pizza dough

4¼ cups all-purpose flour, divided

1 package (2¼ teaspoons) fast-acting dry yeast

2 teaspoons kosher salt

1¼ cups warm water

¼ cup extra-virgin olive oil, plus more for the bowl

cornmeal, for the pizza peel

Combine 1 cup of the flour, yeast, salt, and warm water in the bowl of a food processor with the bread mixing blade. Pulse to mix, then let stand for 10 minutes to allow yeast to dissolve in the slurry.

Add remaining 3½ cups flour and olive oil and mix until a tight ball forms. The dough should feel soft and just a little sticky. If it feels grainy or dry, add warm water, 1 tablespoon at a time, until it reaches the desired consistency.

Dump the dough onto a floured surface and knead by hand until it becomes elastic and springy, about 5 minutes. Knead for another 2 minutes by hand. Transfer to a lightly oiled bowl that's at least twice the size of the dough ball and cover with a damp dish towel. Let the dough rise at room temperature until almost doubled, about 1 hour. The dough is ready when it holds the impression of a finger poked into it.

Place a pizza stone in a cold gas grill and heat to at least 500 degrees, about 1 hour.

Punch down the dough to remove the air and divide it into 8 balls, each about ½ cup in size. Place each ball on a floured surface, and use a rolling pin to roll into rounds. Transfer dough to a pizza peel sprinkled with cornmeal so the dough doesn't stick. Add desired toppings (see Kurt's Pizza Sauce recipe, page 69) to the dough, leaving a ½-inch ring around the edge plain.

Slide the dough onto the preheated pizza stone in the very hot grill. When the bottom has browned and developed strong grill marks and the cheese has melted it is done.

Kurt's Pizza Sauce

Makes approximately 3 cups

This is a quick and easy pizza sauce that tastes garden fresh when made with ripe tomatoes but works just as well with canned. I like to use the sauce sparingly, three table-spoons for a twelve- to fourteen-inch pie, to keep the crust from becoming heavy or soggy. I recommend keeping the toppings simple. With just two or three ingredients you'll taste each one, and the freshness of the pizza sauce will come through.

1 (28-ounce) can crushed tomatoes or 8 Roma tomatoes

2 tablespoons extra-virgin olive oil

2 cloves garlic

1 teaspoon kosher salt

1 teaspoon granulated sugar

¼ teaspoon crushed red pepper

Blend ingredients in a food processor or blender. This recipe will stay fresh in the refrigerator for 5–7 days, or freeze for up to 3 months.

PIZZA TOPPING IDEAS

My mother-in-law's favorite is margherita pizza with just a few slices of fresh mozzarella, then fresh basil leaves spread over the pie when it comes off the pizza stone (always toss fresh herbs on the pie *after* cooking).

BBQ Chicken Pizza
Sauce: barbecue
Toppings: chicken, red onion, mozzarella, chopped cilantro garnish

Margherita
Sauce: olive oil
Toppings: mozzarella, cherry tomato halves, fresh basil garnish

Taco
Sauce: Tapatío hot sauce mixed with tomato sauce
Toppings: cheese, pickled jalapeño, onion, taco meat, or black beans; chopped cilantro and whole tortilla corn chips for garnish

Caramelized Onion
Sauce: olive oil
Toppings: caramelized onions, Parmesan cheese, thyme leaves

Pesto
Sauce: basil pesto
Toppings: mozzarella and cherry tomato halves

Cilantro Pesto
Sauce: Cilantro Pesto (page 80)
Toppings: fresh ricotta and cherry tomato halves or grilled zucchini

Lemony Grains with Herbs

Serves 4

This side dish is terrific with grilled meats and works well with any grains you have in the cupboard. In this recipe I use farro, but you can also use quinoa, rice, millet, or couscous.

1 cup whole farro (not pearled or semi-pearled)

1 orange or yellow bell pepper, chopped

1 cucumber, chopped

½ cup roughly chopped parsley (packed)

¼ cup roughly chopped fresh dill

zest of 1 lemon

⅓ cup fresh lemon juice

¼ cup extra-virgin olive oil

2 teaspoons Dijon mustard

1 teaspoon kosher salt

1 teaspoon black pepper

1 cup feta crumbles

Fill a medium pot halfway with water and bring to a boil. Add the farro, reduce the heat, and simmer until the farro is tender and chewy but still has an al dente bite, about 40 minutes. Drain, then spread the farro onto a large plate or baking sheet to cool for 20 minutes. (This step keeps it from continuing to steam, which makes it mushy.)

In a large bowl, combine cooled grain, bell pepper, cucumber, parsley, dill, and lemon zest. In a small jar, shake together lemon juice, olive oil, mustard, salt, and pepper. Pour dressing over the grains and vegetables. Stir in feta crumbles, and toss to mix thoroughly. Serve warm or at room temperature. Salad will keep 5–7 days in the refrigerator.

Oven-Roasted Potatoes

Serves 4

We spend lots of time talking about food on the island. With our morning coffee, we usually gather around the dining room table or on the dock and talk about the meals for the day. When I first participated, I thought, *Who spends this much time talking about food?* Now I tend to spearhead the conversation. No matter what my meal plan entails, my husband, Kurt, will ask about the starch — a meal isn't a meal to him without protein and starch (he couldn't care less about anything green). The starch could be corn, beans, rice, or other grains, but at his core, he's a meat and potatoes guy. These oven-roasted potatoes are easy, and we usually have potatoes on hand when we need to find a starch for Kurt.

2 pounds Yukon Gold potatoes, cut into 2-inch chunks

3 tablespoons extra-virgin olive oil

2 teaspoons kosher salt

1 teaspoon freshly ground black pepper

2 tablespoons chopped fresh hearty herbs (rosemary, thyme, sage, oregano), optional

parsley, mint, dill, lemon zest, grated Parmesan cheese, for garnish, optional

Heat oven to 425 degrees. Line a large, rimmed baking sheet with parchment paper or a nonstick mat. Place sliced potatoes on the prepared baking sheet, drizzle with oil, then sprinkle with salt and pepper and seasonal herbs, if using. Arrange the potatoes in an even layer. Roast for 30–40 minutes, until golden brown, shaking the pan halfway through the cooking time to redistribute the potatoes. If desired, garnish with less woody herbs like chopped parsley, mint, or dill; lemon zest; or grated Parmesan cheese.

Ribeye Rub

Makes approximately 1 cup

Ribeye is our favorite cut of steak to grill throughout the summer. We like that it's a fattier cut that caramelizes and stays moist and juicy. Let your steaks come to room temperature, and season about 30 minutes prior to grilling to let the meat dry out a bit, which optimizes the caramelization. Julia Child's magic formula for seasoning is a tablespoon of seasoning per pound of meat. I *always* do what Julia says.

3 tablespoons kosher salt

3 tablespoons smoked paprika

3 tablespoons ground coffee

2 tablespoons garlic powder

2 tablespoons crushed red pepper

2 tablespoons onion powder

1 tablespoon cumin

1 tablespoon ground mustard

2 teaspoons cayenne

Combine all ingredients, mixing well. Store any leftover rub in an airtight container.

Roasted Carrots with Scallion-Ginger Sauce

Serves 4

This scallion-ginger sauce recipe is adapted from Francis Lam and *The Splendid Table* radio show. The recipe makes one cup, but you'll only use a quarter of it for this recipe; reserve the rest in the refrigerator or freezer. The sauce will keep in the refrigerator for about two weeks and is excellent served with roasted meats, eggs, fish, or potatoes.

For sauce

1 (3- to 4-inch piece) fresh ginger, cut into ½-inch chunks (no need to peel)

1 small bunch green onions, trimmed, white and light green parts cut into 1-inch pieces

2 teaspoons kosher salt, plus more to taste

½ cup extra-virgin olive oil

For carrots

1 pound carrots, trimmed, cut into 2-inch batons

1 tablespoon extra-virgin olive oil

1 teaspoon kosher salt

freshly ground black pepper

For sauce

Place the ginger, green onions, and salt in a food processor. Pulse until the mixture is combined but still rough. Scrape mixture into a heat-proof bowl and set the bowl over a trivet or hot pad. Heat ½ cup oil in a cast iron pan on high heat until it begins to smoke. Carefully pour the oil over the ginger-onion mixture, stir, and set aside to cool.

For carrots

Heat oven to 400 degrees. Toss carrots with oil, salt, and pepper and spread out on a rimmed baking sheet. Roast carrots for 30 minutes, until cooked through and brown in some spots. Arrange on a platter and spoon ¼ cup scallion-ginger sauce on top (refrigerate remaining sauce for other uses).

Cherry Tomato Tart with Fresh Ricotta and Herbs

Serves 6-8

Fresh ricotta is life changing. Once you've mastered it, you'll use it on toast, pizza, crackers, pasta, and more. If you don't have cheesecloth, a kitchen towel will do. Fresh-made ricotta shines in this simple tart with cherry tomatoes and herbs.

For ricotta
4 cups whole milk

2 cups heavy cream

½ teaspoon kosher salt

3 tablespoons distilled white vinegar

2 tablespoons finely chopped Italian flat-leaf parsley

1 tablespoon finely chopped fresh spring chives

1 teaspoon lemon zest

For tart
1 sheet frozen puff pastry (from a 17.3-ounce box), thawed in the fridge for several hours

4 cups cherry or grape tomatoes

1 tablespoon oil

kosher salt and freshly ground black pepper or crushed red pepper, to taste

1 tablespoon julienned basil

For ricotta
Line a large sieve or colander with a layer of heavy-duty (fine-mesh) cheesecloth and place it over a large bowl.

Slowly bring milk, cream, and salt to a rolling boil in a large, heavy pot over moderate heat, stirring occasionally. Add vinegar, then reduce heat to low and simmer, stirring constantly, until the mixture curdles, about 2 minutes.

Pour the mixture into the lined sieve and let drain for 1 hour (resist the urge to squeeze out excess liquid). Discard the liquid. Mix parsley, chives, and lemon zest into the ricotta. Set in the refrigerator to chill while you prepare the tart crust.

For tart
Heat oven to 375 degrees. On a parchment-lined surface, use a rolling pin to roll puff pastry flat to 9 by 13 inches or so. Slide parchment sheet with rolled pastry onto a 9x13–inch baking sheet. With a straight edge (such as the rolling pin) to guide you, use a knife to score the pastry about 1 inch from the outside edge, making a 1-inch picture frame–like edge. Be careful not to cut all the way through. Prick the pastry inside the entire picture frame with a fork (the pricked area will not rise as much as the outside framed edge, leaving a receptacle for the filling). Bake for 12–15 minutes, until golden brown. If the pastry puffs up inside the edge, gently poke it with a knife point to deflate.

To assemble
Heat broiler to high. In a large bowl, mix tomatoes, oil, salt, and pepper. Transfer to a rimmed baking sheet and broil, shaking pan once or twice, until tomatoes are blistered and have begun to release their juices, 12–14 minutes. Set aside.

Turn the oven to 400 degrees. Spread ricotta mixture on baked tart shell. Use a slotted spoon to transfer the tomato mixture to the prepared tart shell. Distribute tomatoes evenly in a single layer, being careful not to include too much juice. Sprinkle with basil. Return the tart to the oven and bake until hot, about 15 minutes. Let cool slightly before cutting. Tart can be served hot or close to room temperature.

Grandma Bea's Beans

Serves 8-10

My Grandma Bea's baked beans, with bacon, brown sugar, and three types of beans, are super sweet and a real crowd pleaser for large meals or a potluck. Polish Delights, the perfect accompaniment to Grandma Bea's beans, come from Ely's local super-market, Zup's. The Polish Delights recipe began with great-grandpa Joe Zupancich in the 1900s. These Polish-style, hot dog–size sausages are hardwood smoked for more than seven hours, becoming juicy and deli-cious with the perfect snap. Serve grilled Polish Delights in toasted buns with plenty of mustard and sauerkraut. You can buy Zup's sausages online at Zups.com or substitute your favorite smoked sausages here.

8 strips bacon, cut into small pieces

3 large onions, cut into thin rings

4 cloves garlic, chopped

¼ cup distilled white vinegar

¾ cup packed brown sugar

1 teaspoon Dijon mustard

1 (16-ounce) can kidney beans, rinsed and drained

1 (16-ounce) can butter beans, rinsed and drained

1 (53-ounce) can pork and beans

grilled smoked sausages, buns, relishes, for serving

Heat oven to 375 degrees. Brown bacon and onion rings on medium heat for about 5 minutes. Before the bacon becomes crisp, add the garlic, vinegar, brown sugar, and mustard. Cook on medium-low for another 15 minutes, until the onions become caramelized, stirring occasionally. In a large casserole or Dutch oven, combine the beans. Pour the saucy onion mixture over the top of the beans. Bake, uncov-ered, for 1½ hours. Serve with grilled smoked sausages and all the fixin's.

TIP: You can assemble the beans up through the baking step, freeze, and cook later. If you bake from frozen, increase baking time by about 45 minutes.

Mojo Pulled Pork

Serves 8-10

Every cabin needs a great pulled pork recipe. This version is a brighter treatment than the traditional barbecued pork I use for sandwiches. The pulled pork can be served with corn tortillas or chopped into chunks and served over rice on a platter drizzled with the tangy mojo sauce.

For marinade

2 heads garlic, peeled, cloves left whole

2 tablespoons kosher salt

2 teaspoons coarse black pepper

2 tablespoons chopped fresh oregano

zest and juice from 1 orange

zest and juice from 1 lemon

zest and juice from 1 lime

1 (6- to 8-pound) pork shoulder

For serving
corn tortillas

Grilled Onion and Avocado Guacamole (page 58)

Red Cabbage Slaw (page 66)

Cilantro-Orange Rice (page 79)

For marinade
Combine peeled garlic, salt, pepper, and oregano in a food processor and pulse until chopped. Transfer mixture to an extra-large zip-top bag or a bowl that the pork will fit in. Add citrus zests and juices. Reserve ¼ cup of marinade. Add pork to remaining marinade and refrigerate for 8 hours or overnight.

For pork
Let pork come to room temperature for about 1 hour before cooking. Heat gas grill to 325–350 degrees. Cook over indirect heat without flipping for 6–8 hours, until internal temperature registers 190–200 degrees. Transfer the pork to a cutting board, tent with foil, and let sit for about 1 hour before serving.

Pour any juices from the cutting board into the reserved ¼ cup marinade. Heat in a small saucepan until it comes to a low simmer. Meanwhile, use your hands to break up the meat and pull it into chunks you can place on a platter. Top the pulled meat with the heated mojo sauce and serve with corn tortillas, grilled onion guacamole, red cabbage slaw, and cilantro-orange rice.

Molasses Pork Chops

Serves 4

I love thick-cut pork chops that come from small farms with heritage breeds. (No one believes me, but I swear I can smell and taste the ammonia used in the processing of commercially raised pigs.) This marinade lends itself to a juicy chop that holds up well on the grill without drying out. I like to serve these chops with Cilantro-Orange Rice (page 79). If you can find good peaches, grill and present them alongside the chops. Peaches pair very well with pork.

1 cup leftover brewed coffee

⅓ cup dark molasses

2 tablespoons maple syrup

1 tablespoon vinegar (apple cider vinegar preferred; distilled white vinegar works too)

1 tablespoon Dijon mustard

1 large clove garlic, minced or grated

2 teaspoons fresh thyme leaves

1 teaspoon kosher salt

1 teaspoon freshly ground black pepper

1 teaspoon ground ginger

4 bone-in, thick-cut pork chops

Combine the coffee, molasses, maple syrup, vinegar, mustard, garlic, thyme, salt, pepper, and ginger in a large zip-top bag, shaking to combine. Add the pork chops and turn to cover in marinade. Marinate in the refrigerator for at least 2 hours or overnight.

Heat grill to medium-high. Pour the marinade into a bowl for basting the pork. Grill the pork chops for 3–4 minutes, then flip and glaze with the marinade. Cook until chops reach an internal temperature of 145 degrees. Let rest for 5 minutes. Serve glazed side up.

Cilantro-Orange Rice

Serves 4

This rice pairs beautifully with Mojo Pulled Pork (page 77) or as a side dish for fish tacos or grilled chicken.

4 tablespoons butter

½ cup finely chopped onion

1¼ cups orange juice

⅔ cup water

2 tablespoons orange zest, divided

1 teaspoon kosher salt

¼ cup chopped cilantro leaves plus 1 teaspoon finely chopped cilantro stems

1 cup long-grain white rice

Melt the butter in a medium saucepan over medium heat. Add the onions and cook until translucent and tender, about 4 minutes. Add the orange juice, water, 1 tablespoon orange zest, salt, and cilantro stems. Bring the mixture to a boil and add the rice, stir, then cover the pan. Reduce heat to low and simmer for 18–20 minutes, until all the liquid has evaporated and the rice is cooked through. Fluff with a fork. Stir in cilantro leaves and remaining 1 tablespoon orange zest.

Cilantro Pesto Pasta

Serves 4

When Ellie was a little girl, my mother said she always smelled like garlic. She did. We fed pesto to Ellie almost every day, and pesto is chock-full of garlic. This cilantro pesto is a little different take on the traditional basil pesto. I usually prepare it early in the summer because cilantro is one of the first herbs to come up in the garden and bolts quickly. Pesto is best stored frozen in ice cube trays. Pop a cube into soup or thaw a few cubes for a pizza sauce or to mix with mayonnaise and lemon juice to make a pesto aioli.

1 (16-ounce) package farfalle

2 cups packed cilantro, including stems

½ cup raw unsalted walnuts

4 cloves garlic

1 teaspoon kosher salt

½ teaspoon crushed red pepper

⅓ cup extra-virgin olive oil

2 cups cherry tomatoes, halved

Parmesan cheese, for serving

Bring a large pot of salted water to a boil. Add the pasta and return water to a boil. Cook pasta for 8–10 minutes, or until al dente. Reserve ¼ cup pasta water; drain pasta and set aside.

In a food processor, pulse the cilantro, walnuts, garlic, salt, and crushed red pepper until well blended. With the food processor running, drizzle olive oil through the tube and process to combine.

Pour pesto over farfalle and toss with tomatoes. If the mixture seems dry, add pasta water as needed. Serve with Parmesan cheese.

Cast Iron Skillet Roasted Radishes

Serves 4 as a side dish

Radishes are one of the first vegetables to be harvested from our Ely Hilltop Garden. I slice them to add to salads, quick pickle the slices for tacos or rice bowls, or eat them raw dipped in salt. When roasted, as here, the radishes take on a starchy quality almost like a potato. But to my meat-and-potatoes husband, roasted radishes don't qualify as a starch. You be the judge.

2 pounds red radishes (about 40, depending on size), rinsed, trimmed, halved or quartered

1 tablespoon extra-virgin olive oil

1 teaspoon fresh thyme leaves plus 4 sprigs fresh thyme

1 teaspoon cracked black pepper

1 teaspoon kosher salt

Heat oven to 425 degrees. In a cast iron or oven safe skillet, toss radishes with olive oil, thyme leaves, pepper, and salt. Roast for 20–25 minutes, until tender and slightly browned. Garnish with fresh thyme sprigs.

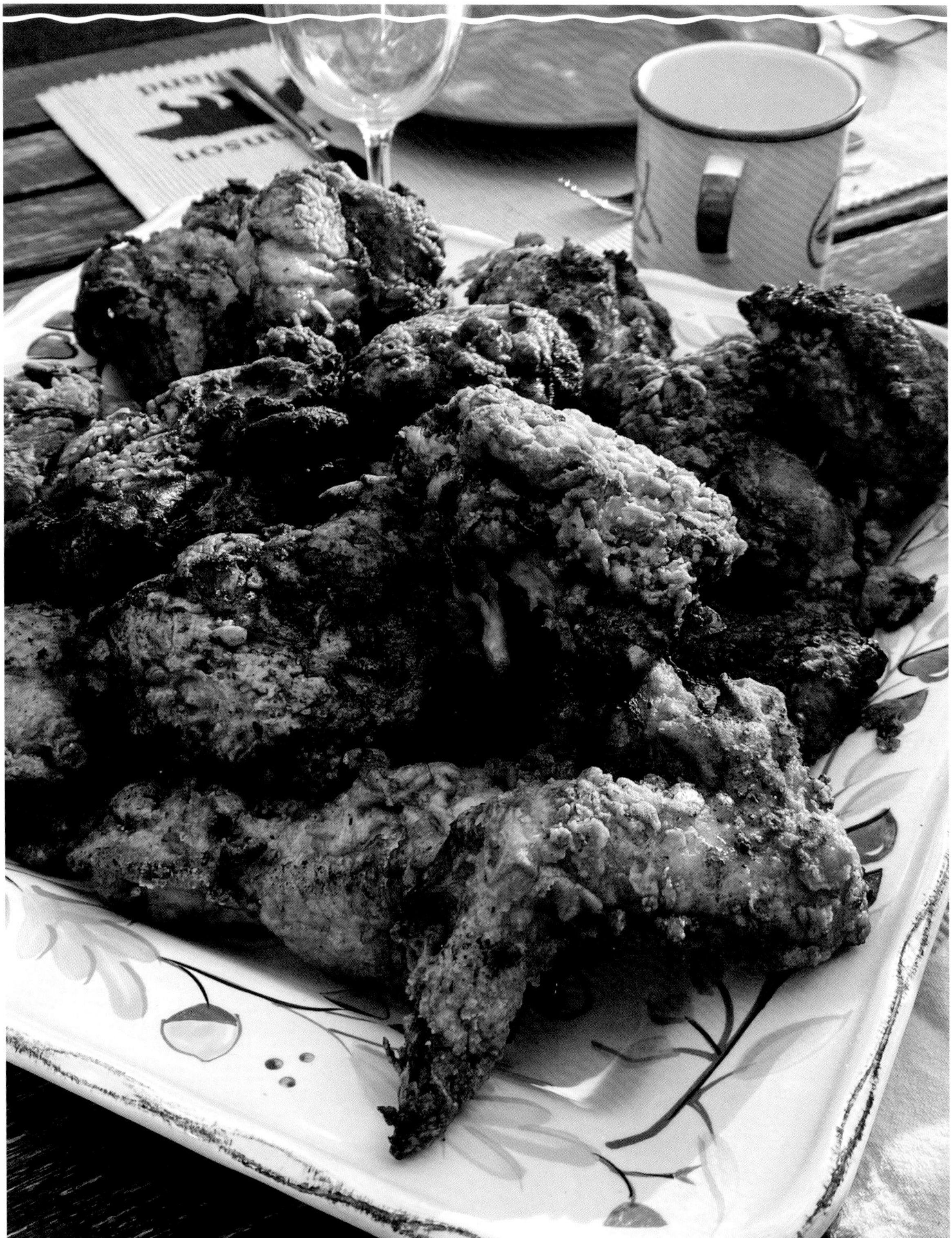

Fried Picnic Chicken

Serves 4-6

My mom made great fried chicken. She shook the chicken pieces in a brown paper grocery bag with flour and black pepper and then pan fried them in a shallow skillet with about half an inch of oil. She used a mesh screen to keep the hot oil from splattering and burning her arms, but I don't remember her frying chicken without getting at least one minor burn. Mom's chicken was light and always served with a pile of mashed potatoes and gravy and a side of Green Giant corn niblets. I like the fried chicken meat, but the crispy skin is my favorite part, so my treatment has a heavier breading to provide optimal crunch. I often double the recipe for a larger group or to have extra for a picnic the next day.

1 organic whole chicken, cut into pieces (see tip)

2 cups (1 pint) buttermilk

1 cup pickle brine from a jar of pickles

8 dashes hot sauce (Tabasco)

2 cups all-purpose flour

1 tablespoon smoked paprika

2 teaspoons kosher salt, plus more for sprinkling

1 teaspoon cayenne

1 teaspoon ground sage

½ teaspoon black pepper

2 cups vegetable oil, for frying

Place chicken pieces in a large 9x13–inch casserole dish. Mix buttermilk, pickle juice, and hot sauce, pour over chicken, and allow to soak for at least 1 hour (up to overnight) in the refrigerator.

Line a baking sheet with parchment paper. Combine flour, paprika, salt, cayenne, sage, and pepper in a large zip-top bag. Add chicken pieces to the bag, 1 at a time, and shake to coat. Lay coated pieces on prepared baking sheet and let sit for 15 minutes to allow the coating to dry a bit.

Heat oven to 200 degrees. Place a wire rack on top of a baking sheet. In a Dutch oven, heat 1 inch of oil over medium heat until it reaches 350 degrees. Without crowding the pot, fry chicken, 2–3 pieces at a time, uncovered, turning once, until coating is dark golden brown and meat is no longer pink, 7–8 minutes per side. Place finished chicken pieces on prepared baking sheet and keep warm in the oven. Sprinkle with kosher salt to taste, and serve on a platter.

TIP: Cut the breasts in half to create smaller pieces for frying.

Beer Can Chicken

Serves 4-6

The idea behind beer can chicken is to stand the chicken upright on a can of beer over the grill so it cooks and browns evenly, and the bird becomes infused with beer flavor. But let's be honest, even an excellent dark stout is unlikely to add any flavor to chicken cooked this way, and furthermore, why waste a good beer? What I do like about beer can chicken is that as it sits upright, the fat renders out slowly, leading to super crispy skin and an evenly browned bird. We use a propane three-burner Weber grill with only the back burner on. We like to add a smoky flavor by placing soaked wood chips in a tray on top of the back burner, then sealing up the rear vent on the grill with a crumpled strip of aluminum foil. We rub the chicken with seasoning and stand it up on the can, then cook it indirectly over the front two burners low and slow for two to three hours. Watch for when the deep brown and crispy skin of the leg just begins to pull away from the end joint. Go for overcooked rather than under-cooked. I guarantee the meat won't dry out and in fact will be extra fla-vorful from the rub. If you use a can of good stout, drink the beer first and then fill the can with tap water. The flavoring is in the chicken, the rub, and the smoke. Enjoy your beer!

1 organic roasting chicken

¼ cup Grilled Chicken Rub (below)

1 tablespoon extra-virgin olive oil

2 teaspoons kosher salt

1 (16-ounce) can beer, for drinking

Heat grill to 300 degrees. Rinse chicken and pat dry with paper towels. Mix chicken rub with oil and salt to make a thick paste. Generously apply the paste to the outside of the chicken. Place a beer can ¾ full (with beer or water) into a chicken rack (if you don't have a roasting stand, use the can alone: just be sure to balance the chicken properly). Place chicken on can. Grill over indirect heat for 2–3 hours until crispy, checking upper thigh for internal temperature of 165 degrees.

Grilled Chicken Rub

Makes about ½ cup

This rub is great on Beer Can Chicken or grilled chicken breasts and thighs. It can also be used on pork chops or pork shoulder.

¼ cup dark brown sugar

1 tablespoon kosher salt

1 tablespoon smoked paprika

2 teaspoons black pepper

2 teaspoons garlic powder

2 teaspoons onion powder

2 teaspoons cayenne

1 teaspoon ground mustard

½ teaspoon ground cinnamon

Mix and store ingredients in a pint-size Mason jar.

Jacobs' Noodles

Serves 8

Back in 1969 my husband's father bought a lot on Lost Girl Island with his friend Dr. Jacob. Kurt had been best friends with Dr. Jacob's three sons and, as Dr. Jacob tells it, was over at their home just about every Saturday to mooch off their weekly pot of cottage cheese and sour cream noodles. Dr. Jacob grew up an only child in San Francisco with his single Jewish mother. I'm guessing this recipe started as a classic Jewish noodle kugel but was quickly consumed by young Harry before his mother could put it in a baking dish and finish it in the oven. The Jacobs continue to make this simple recipe like other families make Kraft macaroni and cheese. The Jacobs still have their place at Lost Girl Island on Burntside Lake, and Kurt still goes over on Saturdays to mooch some sour cream and cottage cheese noodles.

1 (12-ounce) package egg noodles

1¼ cups large curd, full-fat cottage cheese (see tip)

1¼ cups full-fat sour cream

1 teaspoon kosher salt

2 teaspoons freshly ground black pepper

Cook noodles according to package instructions, drain, and add back to the saucepan. Add cottage cheese, sour cream, salt, and pepper to the noodles and stir until everything is incorporated.

TIP: Very important: if you don't use full-fat cottage cheese and sour cream, your noodles will be runny.

NOTE: One Jacob brother adds a bit of milk, cream, or half-and-half to loosen up the noodles a bit. Another Jacob brother adds chives if he has them, and the third Jacob brother doesn't change a thing.

Strawberry Shortcake Drop Biscuits

Serves 6

Making biscuits is no joke. The folks who do it well have the technique down and tend to make biscuits often. Each biscuit maker has their tips and tricks for fluffy, buttery biscuits. I, however, love drop biscuits. Drop biscuits work great for shortcake recipes with juicy summer fruits. The crispy outside of the craggy biscuit holds up much better than the traditional sponge cake often used in strawberry shortcake recipes. I like how the juicy berries and sauce melt into the biscuit center when it's cut open but don't make it soggy. Dough dropped by the spoonful on a baking sheet bakes into a shaggy, unrefined, crispy biscuit, making for a super easy and delicious dessert served with summer berries.

4 cups sliced strawberries

4 teaspoons granulated sugar, divided

1 cup all-purpose flour

2 teaspoons baking powder

½ teaspoon kosher salt

4 tablespoons unsalted butter, chilled, cubed

¼ cup plain Greek yogurt

⅓ cup milk

sweetened whipped cream, for serving

Mix strawberries with 2 teaspoons sugar and refrigerate while juices develop, at least 30 minutes.

Heat oven to 450 degrees. In a bowl, stir together flour, baking powder, remaining 2 teaspoons sugar, and salt. Add cold butter cubes and mix with a fork, pressing the butter against the bowl to break it into pea-size pieces. Add yogurt and milk and stir.

Spray a baking sheet with nonstick cooking spray. Use a large spoon or ¼-cup measure to drop 6 scoops of the biscuit mixture onto prepared baking sheet. Bake for 15 minutes, until golden brown. Serve each biscuit with ½ cup strawberry mixture and sweetened whipped cream.

DOG STORIES

Dogs can be surrogate children, especially when two people are considering a life together. After Kurt and I met at the Heartthrob Café in St. Paul and spent those first few days on True North Island, he was transferred to Baltimore to open a nightclub called Surfside Sally's in the historic district of Fell's Point near the Inner Harbor. I packed up and moved with him. We rented a garden-level apartment in a renovated canning factory and set up house. I got a job selling classified ads for the local weekly entertainment newspaper. From one ad I learned of a litter of puppies for sale. Sophie, a yellow Lab with a crooked nose, was our first child. Sophie was not a great dog for an apartment. She ate the carpet, the kitchen cupboards, part of a closet door, and any pair of shoes she could get her paws on. After a year in Baltimore, we moved back to Minneapolis, leaving behind our security deposit for the copious repairs.

But True North Island is dog heaven. Three acres of forest to roam freely with the natural fencing of water. Run around, chase red squirrels, dig for voles, fetch sticks, poop wherever, swim whenever, and then come home when called for dinner. Sophie, like all our dogs, could smell Burntside Lake as we got near and would come alive in the back seat of our car, standing and panting as we turned onto Grant McMahan Boulevard, the road that leads to the marina at Burntside Lodge.

Sophie had seven wonderful years on the island before she died there. It happened during the cold winter month of February after we'd crossed the frozen lake on cross-country skis pulling a child's sled to ferry our clothes, wine, and food. Kurt chopped a hole in the two-foot-thick ice for water, and we heated the small cabin with the wood-burning stove. Outside the nighttime temperatures were twenty below zero, and inside the fifty-degree temperature was tolerable with a few layers of clothing. The single-pane windows dripped with condensation from the fire and then froze by morning, frosted over like a scene from *Doctor Zhivago*. Sophie loved winters on the lake as much as summers, and the next day she ran alongside as we skied up a

Sophie

frozen river, crossed a portage back to Burntside Lake, and then returned home. We stoked the fire in the cabin and fed Sophie. Then she scratched the door to be let outside. An hour later she still hadn't returned. Kurt found her deep underneath the cabin. She wouldn't come out. We later learned that dogs leave the pack and go off to be alone when they know they're sick or going to die.

To us, it felt like Sophie didn't want her human family to be burdened with the ravages of sickness and death, but in reality dogs instinctively know when they're weak and seek protection from predators — in caves or dens or, in Sophie's case, the tight space underneath the cabin. Kurt crawled in and brought Sophie out. The sun had set, the temperature had dropped to well below zero, and we were miles from our car with only skis for transportation. There was no phone to call for help. We settled her near the woodstove hoping she'd recover. Sophie had a history of seizures, and we suspected another seizure could be coming on. Later that night her breathing slowed and finally stopped. We said our goodbyes to Sophie, and then Kurt carried her outside and placed her body beneath the dock on the clear ice. We spent the rest of that long night in grief.

How did she die? Our vet thought maybe she'd had a heart attack or had complications from her epilepsy, but we never did find out. The next day we would have had difficulty transporting her body back across the frozen lake in the sled, to the car, then back to Minneapolis. We called our local caretaker and asked if he could dispose of the body somewhere on the lake, which was her favorite place. In retrospect maybe this was something we shouldn't have done, and maybe it was even illegal. At the time we weren't thinking clearly, and it seemed like our only option. Our caretaker sent a bill for the job, but we never knew where her body was taken. I guess we assumed into the woods somewhere, buried under a pile of rocks. But in the backs of our minds the thought was always there that maybe he did nothing, and that come spring our dog's body would be there in the water, drifting up against the rocks — that Sophie floats, like Sorrow floats in the book *The Hotel New Hampshire*. We had our eyes peeled to the shore that whole spring and summer, wondering if we would find the remains of our beloved Sophie. We never did.

Simon was a black Lab mixed with spaniel. He was part of a litter that shared a kennel in the animal shelter in St. Paul near Como Park. He was maybe only six months old when he smelled the Mississippi River at an off-leash dog park and immediately jumped in and swam. The dog loved water, and he loved sticks. Up on True North Island, Simon would hunt for any stick in the surrounding woods and then drop it at your feet. Sometimes that stick would be more like a log and crush your toes. It was my mother in-law, Dolores, after a few too many logs were dropped on her feet, who taught Simon the command, "Off the deck!" But if *we* stepped off the deck it was time to play. On the dock, if you didn't keep throwing the stick into the water, Simon would simply drop the stick into the water himself. He could play fetch with himself for as long as you were there watching.

Simon was twelve when he became sick on the island over Memorial Day weekend. He became lethargic and wouldn't eat. Then he crawled under the cabin like Sophie had. Kurt had to crawl in and carry him out. We knew it was bad. This time we had cell phones and speedboat access to the shore. I made an appointment with our vet in Minneapolis, and then we headed back to town early on Memorial Day. By then, Kurt and I were past having surrogate canine children and had a real baby of our own. Ellie was an adorable six years old at the time. She had a ragged pixie haircut and was always slightly dirty on the island in her high-top Keds, jeans, and brown Carhartt jacket with vintage motorcycle patches ironed on by her dad. Simon was Ellie's "little brother," and they adored each other. His head was in Ellie's lap as we drove south toward home. Simon became increasingly lethargic, and in Cloquet we stopped at a local park to let him out to go to the bathroom and drink water. I felt his abdomen, which was hard and bloated. I called our vet, who asked me to look at Simon's gums and see if they were pink. They were not pink; they were gray. The vet said this was not a good sign, Simon was likely in shock, and I needed to find a veterinarian in Cloquet immediately.

With my phone, I located an animal shelter just blocks up the road. We got back in the car and drove there. Kurt stayed in the car with Ellie and

Simon

Simon while I knocked on the door. The shelter was closed, but I was hoping someone was inside caring for the animals, someone who might know where we could find a vet. No one came to the door. I walked toward the back to see if there were any cars, and that was when a small, tawny-brown puppy came running up to me and nearly jumped in my arms. No one was in the back of the shelter, and there were no cars parked nearby. I picked up the puppy and headed back to the car. By then Kurt had found an emergency vet, and we drove the four blocks to his clinic. We kept the tawny-brown puppy with us.

The veterinarian did an X-ray that showed Simon was bloated and his stomach was twisted. Simon was older and in shock, and the veterinarian said the chances of him surviving an emergency surgery were extremely low. While Kurt and I were with Simon and the vet, Ellie was outside on the clinic stoop with the puppy. We went out to sit next to her to explain what was happening with Simon. Before either of us could start, Ellie said, "I named her Nikki." Kurt stayed with the puppy while I walked Ellie in to say final goodbyes to her little brother. Ellie lay down with Simon and whispered into his ear. I do not know what she said, and Ellie cannot remember. She cried, just softly, then kissed Simon goodbye. I led her back out to the stoop. Then Kurt and I said our goodbyes and left the vet with the promise to be back the following weekend to collect Simon's ashes, which we planned to sprinkle over Burntside Lake. We left Nikki with the vet, who assured us there were many dogs just like her in the neighborhood. He said he would make sure Nikki was healthy and put her up for adoption at the shelter we'd been at earlier.

We drove home to Minneapolis. The following Tuesday when I picked up Ellie at her after-school program, she showed me a picture she'd drawn. In crayon was a stick figure of a girl between two dogs. Over the girl she'd written, "Ellie," with an arrow pointing to her. Over the larger black dog she had written, "Simon." Over the brown dog she'd written, "Nikki." I knew then that Nikki was our next dog; she had picked us. I called Kurt and then the vet up in Cloquet. Nikki was still there. We'd have to wait another three days to make sure no one claimed the puppy, but assuming no one would, we could pick her up that Friday.

Nikki was some mix of small husky and maybe chocolate Labrador. She'd obviously been taken to the animal shelter in Cloquet, then abandoned in the parking lot when the shelter was closed over Memorial Day weekend. She took to Ellie and me immediately but was scared of Kurt. Later we discovered that Nikki was wary of all men and most likely had been abused by her previous male owner. It took her years to warm up to Kurt and other men, but eventually she did.

Nikki

Like Sophie and Simon before her, Nikki loved True North Island and knew exactly when we were turning off highway 169 onto Grant McMahan Boulevard, headed to the marina at Burntside Lodge that housed our boat. For the first few days on the island she'd get up with the sun and bark to go outside. She'd be running around chasing and sometimes catching red squirrels, then digging through the tree branches to catch and sometimes eat the slow-moving voles.

Nikki's thick coat of dark tawny-brown fur has faded over the years, and she has grayed around her muzzle and paws. She's now an old, weathered dog, much unlike the sleek little fox we first fell in love with. Of course, we've never known her exact birthday, but as I write this story she's at least seventeen — we think. She still loves being on the island and spends most of the summer there. She acts like a puppy the first few hours after arrival, running laps on the island trails and wading into the water. She no longer chases the red squirrels but instead lays on the deck and watches as they sit up and chirp, taunting her.

Three dogs have become part of our family and enjoyed True North as much as we do — maybe more. They've all been great companions, and I think we somehow live vicariously through their joy of the outdoors and the lake surrounding the island. Then, in the evenings, all have found shelter under the dining table on the deck. Sophie loved any scraps, including soiled napkins, that dropped from the table. Simon was partial to meat and bread and would turn away from fruits and vegetables. Nikki goes crazy for chicken but will also take scraps of fat from beef, pork, or lamb. As a rule, we don't feed our pets during mealtimes, but when Dolores puts her hand under the table, we look the other way. Sometimes it's fun to share the love of food with our dog companions.

Blueberry-Basil Margarita

Serves 1

Margaritas are fantastic. A blueberry margarita is *super* fantastic and also seasonal when fresh blueberries dot the bushes on True North Island. You can use blueberries from the store, though they typically lack flavor. Or substitute frozen Maine blueberries, which are the closest approximation to fresh True North Island blueberries in both size and flavor.

¼ cup blueberries, fresh or frozen, plus more for garnish

1 handful fresh basil leaves, torn, plus more for garnish

1 ounce fresh lime juice (about 1 lime)

2 ounces silver tequila

1 ounce orange liqueur (Cointreau)

lime wedges, for salt rim and garnish

kosher salt, for rim

Add the blueberries, torn basil, and lime juice to a cocktail shaker and muddle together, crushing the basil to release the oils. Fill the shaker with ice and add the tequila and orange liqueur. Place the top on the shaker and shake to combine.

Run the cut side of a lime wedge around a rocks glass. Dip the edge of the glass in kosher salt. Add ice to the glass. Strain the contents of the shaker into the glass. Garnish with fresh basil, blueberries, and a lime wedge.

Dilly Lime Gimlet
or An Evening of Regret (if you have more than one)

Serves 1

I love this cocktail. The lime gives the drink its zest but allows the flavor of the spruce gin to shine through. This is an elegant straight-up sipper served in a martini glass, so take your time with it. Don't do what I did on a girls' weekend and make this your cocktail of choice for the evening. You may regret it in the morning. I know I did.

2 ounces spruce gin (Vikre, made in Duluth, Minnesota)

1 ounce bottled lime juice (Rose's)

½ ounce fresh lime juice

3 sprigs fresh dill

Load a shaker with ice. Add gin, bottled lime juice, fresh lime juice, and 2 sprigs fresh dill rubbed between your fingers to release the oils. Shake and strain into a martini or champagne glass. Garnish with remaining fresh dill sprig.

Grandma Kathy's Chicken Phyllo Bundles

Serves 10 as an appetizer

Whenever we visit Wisconsin to see my dad and stepmom, Kathy, she serves these appetizers, and they are always a huge hit. Kathy is a good cook and often has at least six prepared meals in her freezer ready to go. Breaded chicken, lasagna, various casseroles, or cheesy potato dishes in aluminum foil pans line her basement freezer, labeled and dated, covered with press-and-seal, and loaded into zip-top bags. Kathy's favorite part of any meal is the appetizer, so she never visits without bringing one. These chicken phyllo bundles have become one of the family favorites. Of course, she always has some in the freezer so she can toss them on a baking sheet last minute whenever company stops by.

3 tablespoons fresh lemon juice

2 tablespoons extra-virgin olive oil

1 teaspoon finely chopped garlic

1 teaspoon dried oregano

1 pound boneless chicken breast, cut into strips 2 inches wide by ¼ inch thick

1 (16-ounce) box phyllo dough sheets (2 [8-ounce] rolls)

½ cup (1 stick) butter, melted

soy sauce, for serving

In a casserole dish, combine lemon juice, olive oil, garlic, and oregano with the cut chicken and refrigerate overnight to marinate.

Heat oven to 400 degrees. Unwrap phyllo dough and cut each large sheet in half. Cover with a damp dish towel while assembling. Fold one of the rectangles into a two-ply square. Brush with melted butter. Place 1 piece of chicken in the corner of the square and then roll, folding in the edges as you go, to make a bundle about 2 inches by ½ to 1 inch. (Each bundle will be 2–3 bites.) Repeat with remaining phyllo, butter, and chicken.

When each bundle is complete, place seam-side down on a baking sheet. Brush the bundles with butter and bake for 20 minutes. Serve with soy sauce for dipping.

TIP: After assembly, freeze the bundles on a baking sheet, then store in a zip-top bag in the freezer. When ready to bake, brush with butter and bake for 30 minutes at 400 degrees.

Beth's Cowboy Caviar

SERVES 8–10

My sister, Beth, joins us on True North Island each summer for the Hansen Family Weekend. Typically, this is a four-day affair, and the rules are: bring your dog, your beverage of choice, and food for snacks, breakfast, or lunch — we'll handle dinner. Beth's cowboy caviar — a cross between salsa and bean salad — is a favorite. We pull it out at lunch and happy hour until it's gone, which is usually in the evening on day two.

Hansen Family Weekends don't always turn out well. One year we had a fly infestation. Typically we have a few fly hatches throughout the summer. The flies are usually the smaller kind, more of a nuisance than anything, and sometimes we get biters. On this strange year — it happened only once — the flies were big blue ones (Kurt calls them "s***-house flies"). There were thousands of them everywhere, and if you squashed one it left carnage like a crushed rodent. My dad took to sitting on the deck, flyswatter in hand, whacking, then mounding the remains in a death pile (don't ask me!). Another year we had temperatures in the forties and fifties and freezing rain. It was the third week of July! We tried to make the best of it, taking pontoon rides when the rain subsided, and we went into town for the Blueberry Arts Festival, standing in mud with umbrellas to shop the local crafts. You never know what you'll get with the Hansen Family Weekend.

½ cup finely chopped red onion

½ cup chopped celery

2 (15-ounce) cans black-eyed peas, rinsed

1 (15-ounce) can corn, drained

1 green bell pepper, seeded, finely chopped

1 jalapeño, seeded, finely chopped

½ cup chopped cilantro leaves and stems

¼ cup chopped Italian flat-leaf parsley

2 green onions, white and light green parts, chopped

⅓ cup olive oil

¼ cup fresh lemon juice

2 cloves garlic, minced

2 teaspoons granulated sugar

1 teaspoon kosher salt

½ teaspoon black pepper

tortilla or pita chips, for serving

In a large bowl, toss together red onion, celery, black-eyed peas, corn, bell pepper, jalapeño, cilantro, parsley, and green onions. In a separate bowl, stir together olive oil, lemon juice, garlic, sugar, salt, and pepper. Pour dressing over the salad ingredients and stir, then let it marinate for a minimum of 4 hours in the refrigerator. Serve with tortilla or pita chips.

Creamy Coleslaw with Apples

Serves 6

We love a good coleslaw on the island, and this recipe gets a hint of sweetness from grated apple and honey. Usually the Ely Hilltop Garden gives us four to six huge cabbages to use for slaw, Simple Sauerkraut (page 163), and Roasted Cabbage Steaks (page 191) throughout the season.

½ cup plain Greek yogurt

¼ cup mayonnaise

2 tablespoons Dijon mustard

2 tablespoons honey

1 tablespoon apple cider vinegar

1 tablespoon buttermilk (or use milk or cream)

1 teaspoon kosher salt

½ teaspoon black pepper

4–5 cups shredded cabbage (green or a mix of red and green)

1 medium apple, shredded

2 carrots, shredded

In a medium bowl, combine the yogurt, mayonnaise, mustard, honey, vinegar, buttermilk, salt, and pepper, and stir until smooth.

In a large bowl, toss together the cabbage, apples, and carrots. Pour the dressing over the slaw and stir to distribute evenly. Refrigerate until ready to serve.

Corn Skillet

Serves 6

I think this recipe first appeared at the cabin when Ellie had braces on her teeth. There's nothing worse than your kid picking corn out of their braces at the dinner table. I love all the fresh flavors in this recipe, with the ginger, lime juice, and herbs to finish. If you're out of cilantro, use mint, basil, or parsley.

4 tablespoons unsalted butter

1 cup thinly sliced green onions, white and light green parts

2 tablespoons grated fresh ginger

1 tablespoon minced garlic

1 jalapeño, seeded and finely chopped

5 cups fresh corn kernels (about 6 ears of corn; see tip)

¼ cup chopped cilantro

¼ cup fresh lime juice

1 teaspoon kosher salt

freshly ground black pepper

Melt butter in a large skillet or Dutch oven over medium heat. Add the green onions and cook, stirring, for 3 minutes. Add the ginger, garlic, and jalapeño, and cook, stirring, for 2 minutes more. Add the corn to the skillet and cook for 4 minutes, stirring frequently until the corn is tender. Remove from heat and stir in cilantro, lime juice, salt, and pepper to taste. Serve warm.

TIP: To cut the corn kernels off the husk, anchor the cob in the center of a Bundt pan and run your sharp knife down the cob. All the kernels will fall neatly into the Bundt pan.

Richard's Fried Potatoes

Serves 3-4

To be honest, there's nothing special about this recipe. It is what it is: fried potatoes, and you can use any potatoes, though you might want to peel the russets. What makes this recipe special is that Kurt's father, Richard, used to prepare the fried potatoes along with T-bone steaks over a campfire on the point of True North Island. Richard started this tradition way back when he purchased the island in 1971. The idea was to roast the T-bones over the fire while sliced potatoes were fried in a cast iron skillet of oil. This setup was tricky. The coals, maybe ten inches from the grate, needed to be very hot to cook the meat; then as the steaks cooked, the grease from the rendered fat started up fires that resulted in a severe char. Getting the steaks close to medium-rare proved difficult, and actually one of the traditions was to drown the meat and potatoes in ketchup and Worcestershire sauce because they were always overdone. This overcooked mélange was served with a salad and lots of red wine — Gallo Hearty Burgundy, or so I'm told.

Times have changed. Call me urbane, a snob, or worse, but I prefer a ribeye steak cooked on the grill to medium-rare, not well-charred. If I have the choice, I like eating at our outdoor table with chairs versus balancing my plate on my lap while perched on a tree stump with smoke billowing in my face. What I really like are these fried potatoes alongside my steak. And I'm not above adding ketchup and Worcestershire sauce.

4 Yukon Gold potatoes, cut into ⅛-inch slices

2 cups vegetable oil

1 tablespoon extra-virgin olive oil

1 teaspoon kosher salt

1 teaspoon freshly ground black pepper

Place potato slices in a large saucepan and add cold water to cover. Heat to boiling and parboil for 7–8 minutes. A knife or fork should go in with only slight resistance.

Start a gas grill and set all burners to high. Pour vegetable oil into a 12-inch cast iron skillet. (The oil should come up to ½ inch on the side of the skillet.) Place the skillet on the grill and cover until the oil temperature reaches 375 degrees. Wearing an oven mitt, carefully place potatoes in the skillet (the hot oil will spatter). Cook for about 30 minutes, stirring and flipping the potatoes every 5 minutes. They should be nicely brown with plenty of crispy edges and bits.

Remove potatoes from pan and toss with olive oil, salt, and pepper.

FOREST FIRES

The 1991 blowdown storm flattened every tree in a swath forty miles long and ten miles wide, roughly 500,000 acres. Ellie, Kurt, and I were on the island when it happened (see How the Island Got Its Name, page 49). Almost immediately afterward, there was talk about all that downed timber eventually drying up and becoming tinder for an explosive forest fire. We'd seen a few over the years, some right on Burntside Lake. Everyone in the north woods thinks about forest fires (or should), and we all do what we can to mitigate the possibility. But that awareness didn't come without some hard lessons. In one, we almost burned down our own island.

It was just after Kurt and I were married. We had our friends, Bill and Julia, up for a long weekend. Back then we still had a Weber charcoal grill, and the first night we cooked steaks over briquets. The next afternoon Kurt made the classic mistake of throwing the old ashes in a garbage bag near the trash can at the back of the cabin. Nothing happened until the middle of that second night. I woke up and saw this weird reflection in the sliding glass doors, waving lights of orange and red, and for a moment I thought we'd left a light on somewhere. But then I got up and looked out and saw the island on fire. I screamed, "Fire, fire, fire!"

Kurt woke first, shouting, "What, what, what!?" And I kept shouting, "Fire, fire, fire!" He finally looked out the glass doors. He shot out of bed and ran outside naked. I followed. The flames were ten feet high and covered the area of a small dining room. Soon Bill was outside (thankfully he was wearing shorts), and Julia was right behind him, eight months pregnant with their first child. By then Kurt had gone into the shed and found a bucket, and I went into the cabin and grabbed the plastic kitchen trash can. I took both down to the lake to get them filled. Kurt started up the garden hose, which looked next to useless against the flames that were now spreading into the overhead pine branches. I set the filled bucket on the deck. Julia, who is tiny and was very pregnant, dragged the bucket over to Bill, who threw it on the fire. That seemed to have more impact. I was back with the filled garbage can, and now we had a regular bucket brigade going. At that point I heard Bill say, "It's out of control!"

But the bucket brigade worked. Bill dumped a five-gallon trash can of water on the center of the fire, and that seemed to knock down the flames. And Kurt, still naked, was working the edges of the fire with the garden hose. It took us nearly an hour to put out the fire, but then we could see smoke coming up through the undergrowth of dried moss. We stayed up for another hour just soaking the edges of the scorched black earth with buckets of water and the hose, and at some point Bill told Kurt to go put on some shorts. The sky in the east was starting to lighten when we finally went back to bed, and for two days we left a sprinkler on to keep the ground wet. The next time we came to the island, we replaced the Weber charcoal kettle grill with a propane model. Knock on wood, we've had no other fires.

Kale and Bacon Tart

Serves 12

I am always trying to find ways to use kale from the garden. Kale is one of those crops that grows throughout the summer, so we have lots of it. I love quick-sautéed kale in olive oil with red pepper flakes that you hit with a squeeze of lemon juice and a sprinkle of salt just before serving. Kale paired with bacon is magical, and this kale and bacon tart will please even the pickiest eaters.

4 slices bacon, cut into 1-inch pieces

2 tablespoons extra-virgin olive oil

1 cup chopped yellow or red onion

2 cloves garlic, chopped

6 cups chopped kale

1 teaspoon kosher salt

1 teaspoon black pepper

2 tablespoons heavy cream

1 sheet puff pastry (from a 17.3-ounce package), thawed

½ cup grated Parmesan cheese

Cook bacon pieces in a skillet over medium heat until brown. Remove from the pan and set aside on a piece of paper towel to drain. Wipe bacon fat from the pan and add the olive oil and the onions. Cook the onions over medium heat until they are beginning to caramelize, about 20 minutes. Add the garlic and cook for 1 minute more. Add the kale to the onion mixture and cook until the kale is wilted, about 4 minutes. Add the bacon, salt, and pepper and pour in the cream, stirring to combine. Remove from heat.

Heat oven to 375 degrees. On a parchment-lined surface, use a rolling pin to roll puff pastry flat to 9 by 13 inches or so. Slide parchment sheet with rolled pastry onto a 9x13–inch baking sheet. With a straight edge (such as the rolling pin) to guide you, use a knife to score the pastry about 1 inch from the outside edge, making a 1-inch picture frame–like edge. Be careful not to cut all the way through. Prick the pastry inside the entire picture frame with a fork (the pricked area will not rise as much as the outside framed edge, leaving a receptacle for the filling). Bake for 12–15 minutes, until golden brown. If the pastry puffs up inside the edge, gently poke it with a knife point to deflate. Add the kale mixture inside the picture frame, leaving the surrounding outside inch of dough exposed. Smooth filling and sprinkle on Parmesan cheese.

Bake for 20–25 minutes, until the edges of the tart are golden brown. Cut into squares and serve.

Grammy's Macaroni and Cheese

Adapted from **The Joy of Cooking**

Serves 6

I loved my mother's macaroni and cheese. It was baked in a 2.5-quart dark brown Pyrex casserole dish with white flowers printed on the outside. I loved how the top of the dish would get that crispy brown crust, but the elbow macaroni inside the dish was cheesy and gooey. My mom didn't put bread crumbs on her macaroni and cheese, but I can't resist the buttery topping in the version here. Grammy's Macaroni and Cheese is a favorite on my side of the family and works great as a main dish or as a starchy side with grilled meats and a big green salad or slaw. I always sprinkle my portion with lots of Tabasco.

2 cups elbow macaroni

7 tablespoons butter, divided

2 tablespoons all-purpose flour

1½ cups 2 percent or whole milk

1 bay leaf

1 teaspoon ground mustard

1 teaspoon ground turmeric

1 teaspoon kosher salt

½ teaspoon paprika

2 cups grated sharp cheddar cheese

black pepper, to taste

½ cup panko bread crumbs

Heat oven to 350 degrees. Grease a 1.5- or 2-quart baking dish. Cook pasta in salted boiling water according to the package instructions until al dente.

Melt 2 tablespoons butter in a saucepan and stir in flour. Cook the flour and butter mixture for 3 minutes, stirring constantly. Whisk in the milk, stirring well to prevent lumps. Add bay leaf, mustard, turmeric, salt, and paprika. Simmer, gently whisking, for 10 minutes to make sure everything is incorporated. Remove from heat, discard bay leaf, and stir in the cheese. Season with pepper and additional salt to taste. Stir in cooked macaroni and mix well.

Pour macaroni mixture into the prepared baking dish. Melt 3 tablespoons butter in a small skillet and add panko bread crumbs, coating them with butter and cooking until browned. Sprinkle the browned bread crumbs on top of the casserole. Dot the top of the casserole with chunks of the remaining 2 tablespoons butter. Bake for 30 minutes or until bread crumbs are lightly browned and cheese is bubbly. Let stand for 10 minutes before serving.

Swiss Chard Gratin

Serves 6

Swiss chard is a dream for gardeners. It flourishes in any soil, and it's healthy and tasty. It also grows copiously throughout the summer, leaving me challenged to find ways to cook it so my family will eat chard yet one more night. You can always count on cheese and cream to make anything rich and tasty. Wisconsinites have known this for decades.

4 tablespoons unsalted butter, divided

½ cup bread crumbs

½ cup shredded Parmesan cheese

½ cup chopped white onion

3 cloves garlic, minced

6 handfuls chopped Swiss chard

1 teaspoon kosher salt

1 teaspoon fresh thyme leaves

1 cup heavy cream

scant sprinkling nutmeg

coarse-ground black pepper, to taste

extra-virgin olive oil

Heat oven to 375 degrees. Grease a 1.5-quart baking dish with 1 tablespoon butter.

In a small bowl, stir together bread crumbs and shredded Parmesan cheese. Add in 1 tablespoon butter and mix with your hands to get a crumbly mixture of buttery clumps, like pie dough. Set aside.

Melt 1 tablespoon butter in a skillet over medium heat, then add onions and cook, stirring, for 3 minutes. Add in garlic and cook for another minute. Add the Swiss chard by the handful and cook down until slightly wilted, approximately 3 minutes. Add salt and thyme and stir to combine. Drain any excess liquid from the Swiss chard mixture, then pour mixture into the prepared baking dish. Top with cream and sprinkle with nutmeg. Top with the bread crumb mixture and black pepper to taste. Drizzle olive oil over the top of the bread crumbs and dot with small pieces of the remaining 1 tablespoon butter.

Bake for 12 minutes, until the mixture is bubbly and the top is golden brown. Let rest for 5 minutes, then serve.

Zucchini Fritters with Lemony Yogurt Sauce

Serves 6

When Ellie was a teenager, I asked her to list the recipes I made that she loved. She said, "I don't know; you don't really make anything more than once." She proceeded to rattle off recipes she loved: Dolores's Teriyaki Steak (page 150), Dolores's King Ranch Chicken (page 111), Grammy's Macaroni and Cheese (page 104), Dad's BBQ Ribs (page 118), and so on. My feelings were a bit hurt, but I pressed her to keep going. Finally, she came up with my fritters. I make both corn and zucchini fritters, typically in August, when those vegetables are plentiful and taking over every meal. The yogurt sauce is light and could also be used on potato pancakes or falafel with a bit of grated or chopped cucumbers and a few fresh herbs mixed in.

TIP: If using a very large zucchini that has developed seeds, remove seeds before grating.

For fritters

1½ pounds grated zucchini (4 small, 2 medium, or 1 very large; about 5–6 cups; see tip)

2 teaspoons kosher salt, divided

2 whole green onions, thinly sliced

1 large egg, lightly beaten

2 cloves garlic, minced or grated

1 teaspoon black pepper

1 tablespoon finely chopped parsley

½ cup all-purpose flour

¼ cup finely grated Parmesan cheese

½ teaspoon baking powder

2 tablespoons extra-virgin olive oil or vegetable oil, for frying

For sauce

1 cup plain unsweetened Greek yogurt

1 tablespoon mayonnaise

1 teaspoon lemon zest

1 tablespoon lemon juice

1 teaspoon kosher salt

1 small clove garlic, minced or grated

Corn Fritters

For fritters

Toss zucchini and 1 teaspoon salt together in a large colander and place in the sink to drain for 10 minutes. Dump zucchini onto a clean kitchen towel and wring out as much of the liquid as possible. Transfer zucchini shreds to a large mixing bowl. Add green onions, beaten egg, garlic, pepper, parsley, flour, Parmesan cheese, baking powder, and remaining 1 teaspoon salt to bowl. Mix well.

Heat 2 tablespoons of oil in a cast iron skillet over medium heat. Heat oven to 200 degrees. Scoop scant ¼ cups of batter into the hot skillet to form fritters, being careful not to crowd the pan. Fry until golden brown, about 3 minutes per side. Place cooked fritters on paper towels or newspaper to drain, then transfer to the warm oven until ready to serve.

For sauce

Stir ingredients together. Scoop 1 teaspoon of sauce onto each fritter at the table, or assemble fritters on a pretty platter and drizzle with sauce.

Serves 6

1½ cups all-purpose flour

2 teaspoons baking powder

1 teaspoon kosher salt

1 teaspoon freshly ground black pepper

3 cups fresh corn kernels (from about 3 cobs)

1 green onion, light green and white parts thinly sliced

2 tablespoons chopped fresh dill (or parsley, basil, or cilantro)

1 small clove garlic, minced or grated

½ cup 2 percent milk

2 large eggs, beaten

⅓ cup vegetable oil

Whisk together the flour, baking powder, salt, and pepper in a large bowl. Add corn, green onions, dill, garlic, milk, and eggs and mix well. The batter will be thick; do not overmix. Set aside.

Heat the oil in a cast iron skillet over medium heat. Heat oven to 200 degrees. Scoop scant ¼ cups of batter into the hot skillet to form fritters, being careful not to crowd the pan. Fry until golden brown, about 3 minutes per side. Place cooked fritters on paper towels or newspaper to drain, then transfer to the warm oven until ready to serve.

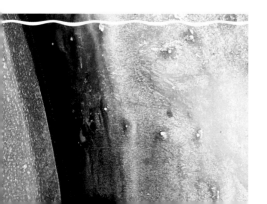

Grammy's Potato Salad

Serves 10–12

Some people love to chop. My mother, Anne, was one of those people. She'd stand in the kitchen in her bathrobe watching her daytime soap operas and chopping and prepping for dinner. I always thought my mom was a great cook. She cooked every night, always a protein, starch, and vegetable. I loved her meat loaf, fried chicken, barbecue meatballs or ribs, and even her chow mein served on fried La Choy noodles — such a treat. My sisters and I thought she made the best mashed potatoes and gravy. She made a meaty chili with elbow macaroni (a Wisconsin thing?). Her perfect mustard-yellow potato salad stood out not only for its deliciousness but also because she was a great chopper — the potatoes and cucumbers were always perfectly cubed, the radishes sliced thin. Frankly, it's not my strength to be super precise, and all that chopping isn't my favorite. I did, however, love making this recipe for the cookbook as it led me down memory lane. Now my sister, Beth, has taken on the tradition of making Grammy's Potato Salad, and she chops as well as our mom did.

For salad

5 pounds large red potatoes

⅓ cup French dressing

2 bundles green onions, thinly sliced

1 cucumber, peeled, seeded, cut into bite-size cubes

1½ cups chopped celery

⅓ cup thinly sliced radishes, divided

¼ cup chopped fresh dill

4 large hard-boiled eggs, sliced (an egg slicer works best)

For dressing

⅓ cup mayonnaise

⅓ cup sour cream

2 tablespoons French's yellow mustard

1 tablespoon horseradish

2 teaspoons kosher salt

1 teaspoon black pepper

1 teaspoon celery salt

1 teaspoon onion salt

For salad

Score the potatoes with an X on each side and add to a pot of water. Heat water to a boil and cook potatoes until just barely cooked through, about 10 minutes. Peel the skins from the potatoes while hot. Place peeled potatoes in a bowl and drizzle with French dressing, tossing to coat. Refrigerate overnight.

Cut the potatoes into bite-size (about ½-inch) cubes. Toss with the green onions, cucumbers, celery, half the radishes, and dill.

For dressing and garnish

Whisk together mayonnaise, sour cream, mustard, horseradish, salt, pepper, celery salt, and onion salt. Pour dressing over the salad and mix gently to avoid breaking up potatoes. Alternate radish slices and egg slices as decorations on top of the salad before serving.

Janice's Potato Salad

Serves 4-6

Aunt Janice is my mother-in-law's sister, and her potato salad has become world famous. Everyone who comes to the island wants this potato salad, and Dolores and I probably make it about ten times each summer. This potato salad is unique in that it's not super heavy, has acidity from lime juice, and involves no eggs. You can substitute fresh dill for the dried, but in this case I think the dried tastes best. Sometimes I use both — the dried dill for flavor and the fresh dill for a lovely garnish. The recipe is *maybe* world famous because I made it live on *The Jason Show* last spring. Janice was thrilled.

1 cup mayonnaise

¼ cup Dijon mustard

1 teaspoon fresh lime juice

½ teaspoon kosher salt

½ teaspoon black pepper

1 tablespoon dried dill (or ¼ cup chopped fresh dill)

2 pounds red potatoes, boiled with skins on and refrigerated for 4 hours

2 green onions, both white and light green parts, sliced

½ cup finely chopped red onion

2 cloves garlic, minced

Mix mayonnaise, mustard, lime juice, salt, pepper, and dill in a cup. Set aside, refrigerated, for at least 2 hours to allow flavors to meld.

Cut chilled potatoes into ½-inch cubes. Place potatoes, green onions, red onion, and garlic in a bowl and toss with dressing to coat. Set aside, refrigerated, to allow flavors to meld.

Dolores's King Ranch Chicken

Serves 6

King Ranch chicken casserole is a popular Tex-Mex dish that came to us on True North Island via mother-in-law Dolores's time working at the Houston Grand Opera. Apparently, the name comes from the King Ranch, which spans more than 800,000 acres and is one of the largest working ranches in the United States. Casserole in Texas isn't that different from hot dish in Minnesota. Cheesy, crusty, and delicious, this King Ranch chicken is a favorite of daughter Ellie and nephew Chris Leer.

2 tablespoons vegetable oil

1 yellow onion, chopped

2 cloves garlic, chopped

4 cups chopped cooked chicken (see tip)

1 (10.5-ounce) can cream of chicken soup

1 (10.5-ounce) can cream of mushroom soup

1 teaspoon chili powder

1 teaspoon kosher salt

4 dashes hot sauce (Tabasco), plus more for serving

12 corn tortillas, torn into 1-inch pieces

2 cups grated cheddar cheese

1 (10-ounce) can diced tomatoes and green chilies (RO*TEL Original), drained

1 (4.5-ounce) can chopped green chiles, drained

chips, cilantro, and sour cream, for serving

Heat oven to 350 degrees. Add the vegetable oil to a large cast iron skillet over medium-high heat and cook onions, stirring often, for 4 minutes. Add the garlic and cook, stirring, for 2 minutes more. Stir in chopped chicken, cream of chicken soup, cream of mushroom soup, chili powder, salt, and hot sauce. Remove from heat.

Layer half of the torn tortillas in the bottom of a lightly greased 9x13–inch baking dish. Top with half the chicken mixture. Add another layer of tortillas and then the remaining chicken mixture. Top with the cheese. Spoon the diced tomatoes and the green chiles over the top. Bake for 1 hour, until cheese is melted and bubbly.

Serve warm with chips, cilantro, sour cream, and hot sauce.

TIP: Dolores blanches 3 breasts or 6 thighs in a pot of water with stock fixings like onions, carrots, and celery. Then she dips the tortillas in the stock to moisten them before assembling the casserole. Feel free to take a shortcut with rotisserie chicken or leftovers from roasted chicken.

Lila's Green Pork Stew

Serves 6

Lila and Harry Jacob, along with Kurt's parents, purchased adjoining island lots on Burntside's Lost Girl Island when they both visited their kids at the canoe camp nearby. Over the years, Lila and Harry became our summer companions. We'd share weekend drinks on their porch overlooking the bay of Lost Girl Island, and Lila would serve olives, crackers (usually saltines), cheese, and sometimes homemade guacamole and chips. The Jacobs had lots of guests throughout the summer, including their three grown boys and their families, and Lila was often saddled with cooking meals for large groups. She did not love cooking. As a respite, I would invite her and Harry over for dinner. She was a wonderful guest and appreciated anything I cooked, even lamb, of which she was not initially a fan. One weekend she had family visiting from Mexico City and Kurt and I were invited over for her green pork stew and cornbread. It was so good and made such an impression on me that I wanted to include the recipes here.

10 medium tomatillos, husked, halved

1 large poblano pepper

2 teaspoons kosher salt, divided

4 cups (1 quart) chicken broth

1 cup packed cilantro leaves

3 tablespoons fresh lime juice (about 1 lime)

2 teaspoons Worcestershire sauce

2½ pounds boneless pork shoulder roast (Boston butt), trimmed and cut into 1-inch pieces

1 teaspoon freshly ground black pepper

3 tablespoons vegetable oil

1 white onion, chopped

4 medium cloves garlic, chopped

rice, tortilla chips, flour tortillas, or cornbread, for serving

radishes, cilantro, green onion, or pickled jalapeño, for garnish

Heat broiler and move an oven rack to 5 inches from the broiler. Cover a baking sheet with aluminum foil. Broil tomatillos and poblano pepper on the prepared baking sheet for 5 minutes, until skins look blistered with some spots of black or brown. Remove from the oven. Place poblano pepper in a zip-top plastic bag, seal, and let stand for 10 minutes to loosen skin. Rub the skin off the poblano pepper; remove and discard seeds.

Place tomatillos, poblano pepper, 1 teaspoon salt, broth, cilantro, lime juice, and Worcestershire sauce in a blender and process until smooth, stopping to scrape down sides as needed (or use a handheld immersion blender).

Sprinkle pork with pepper and remaining 1 teaspoon salt.

Heat a Dutch oven over medium-high. Heat oil, then cook pork in batches, stirring often, about 6 minutes or until the pork is browned on all sides. Add onions and cook, stirring, for 4 minutes. Add garlic and cook, stirring, for 1 minute more. Add blended tomatillo mixture to the pot, stirring to loosen any browned bits from the bottom of the pan. Bring to a light simmer, cover, and reduce heat to medium-low. Cook, stirring occasionally, 1½ hours or until pork is fork tender. Uncover and cook, stirring occasionally, 30 minutes or until liquid is slightly thickened.

Serve with rice, tortilla chips, flour tortillas, or cornbread. Garnish with radishes, chopped cilantro, green onion, and pickled jalapeño.

Lila's Mexican Cornbread

Serves 8

3 large eggs

¾ cup vegetable oil

2 cups sour cream

2 teaspoons kosher salt

2¼ cups cornmeal

4 teaspoons baking powder

2 jalapeños, finely chopped

½ green bell pepper, finely chopped

½ teaspoon chili powder

1 (14.5-ounce) can creamed corn

2½ cups grated sharp cheddar cheese

Heat oven to 350 degrees. In a medium bowl, beat eggs. Add oil, sour cream, and salt, stirring to mix well. In a separate bowl, sift together cornmeal with baking powder. Stir into egg mixture. Add jalapeños, bell pepper, chili powder, and creamed corn. Beat with a wooden spoon until combined.

Grease a 10-inch cast iron skillet and pour in half of the corn batter. Sprinkle on half the grated cheese. Pour the remaining corn batter on top, then add remaining grated cheese. Bake for 45 minutes, until a toothpick inserted into the center comes out clean.

Dolores's Barbecue Brisket

Serves 8–10

This dish is a signature for my mother-in-law, Dolores, who lived in Houston, Texas, for fifteen years. The recipe is adapted from the famous *Treebeards Cookbook*, Treebeards being a restaurant with locations around Houston. Their brisket was reputedly a favorite of former Presidents George H. W. Bush and George W. Bush. The recipe takes a few days to set up, so plan ahead. Serve it alongside Grammy's Macaroni and Cheese (page 104) and Janice's Potato Salad (page 110), as we did for Ellie's open house to celebrate her graduation from high school.

For barbecue sauce

1 cup chopped white onion

2 cloves garlic, minced

1 cup ketchup

½ cup distilled white vinegar (or apple cider vinegar)

½ cup extra-virgin olive oil

¼ cup fresh lemon juice

3 tablespoons Worcestershire sauce

2 tablespoons liquid smoke

2 teaspoons ground mustard

4 shakes hot sauce (Tabasco)

¼ cup brown sugar

2 teaspoons kosher salt

For brisket

¼ cup brown sugar

2 teaspoons celery seed

1 teaspoon paprika

1 teaspoon black pepper

1 teaspoon kosher salt

¼ teaspoon garlic powder

¼ teaspoon crushed red pepper

2 teaspoons liquid smoke

1 (4-pound) beef brisket, trimmed of visible fat

For barbecue sauce

Place all ingredients in a blender or food processor and process until smooth. Transfer to a saucepan, bring to a simmer, cover, and simmer for 30 minutes.

For brisket

In a small bowl, mix brown sugar, celery seed, paprika, black pepper, salt, garlic powder, crushed red pepper, and liquid smoke. Rub the mixture all over the brisket. Place in a zip-top bag and refrigerate overnight.

One hour before cooking, take the brisket out of the refrigerator. Heat grill to 300 degrees. Place brisket in a shallow roasting pan. Cover the pan with aluminum foil and bake for 45 minutes per pound of brisket, until brisket is tender (approximately 3½ hours for a 4-pound roast). Remove from the grill and allow to cool.

One hour before serving, remove the brisket from the pan. Reserve any pan juices. Cut beef against the grain into thin, diagonal slices and arrange in a roasting pan. In a small bowl, mix up to 1 cup pan juices and 1½ cups barbecue sauce. Pour over the sliced brisket.

Heat oven or grill to 325 degrees. Cover the roasting pan with aluminum foil and reheat the brisket in the oven or over indirect heat on the grill for 45 minutes, until the brisket is fork tender. Serve with remaining sauce.

Grandma Bea's Good Beef Sandwiches

Serves 10–12

My dad grew up in Waupaca, Wisconsin. We'd visit two to three times each year, piling all four girls and our pets into a white Pontiac Grand Prix. My sister Beth and I are close in age, and for the whole four-hour drive we fought. I vividly remember using a pillow to create a wall between us to keep her from touching or looking at me. Eventually we made it to Waupaca in one piece, and once there it was a tradition to have Grandma's beef sandwiches with potato rolls. Of course, I complained that we always had the same thing. Now I look forward to making beef sandwiches for the Hansen family up on the island, and — guess what? — I don't even mind driving with my sisters.

¼ teaspoon onion powder

¼ teaspoon paprika

¼ teaspoon garlic powder

¼ teaspoon black pepper

2 cans beef consommé

¼ cup soy sauce

2 tablespoons Worcestershire sauce

1 (8-pound) beef rump roast

4 medium cloves garlic, sliced into slivers

sliced red onion, for serving

potato rolls, for serving

Heat oven to 250 degrees. Whisk together onion powder, paprika, garlic powder, pepper, consommé, soy sauce, and Worcestershire. Cut slits all over roast and push garlic slivers into the slits. Place roast in a roasting pan and cover with the sauce. Cover the pan tightly with aluminum foil and roast for 8–9 hours.

Take the roast out of the pan and wrap in foil. Pour juices into a bowl. Refrigerate roast and juices at least 4 hours or overnight. (The refrigeration time keeps the roast from falling apart when slicing.)

When ready to serve, slice the roast and place in a roasting pan or Dutch oven. Scrape off the fat layer from the reserved juices and discard. Add the defatted juices to the roasting pan with the meat. Reheat meat and sauce. Serve with sliced red onion and potato rolls.

Fried Walleye with Lemony Tartar Sauce

Serves 4

When my husband, Kurt, was younger, he thought the magic spot for catching fish was on a small clump of rocks a few hundred feet off the point of True North Island where seagulls flocked. There he could see the picked bones of large walleye. The gulls guarded the island jealously and would dive-bomb any kid in a boat who came near, like something out of Hitchcock's *The Birds*. One afternoon Kurt and his brother donned plastic baseball batter's helmets and braved the birds. One fished while the other swung a bat overhead as the birds came close. They caught nothing.

It wasn't until years later that Kurt noticed the neighbors trolling out to the same tiny island and throwing fish bones and guts on the rocks. No birds attacked the incoming boat, and the neighbors could get right up to the rocky shore with their bucket of fish guts. Those neighbors still throw their discards on the rocks, and we sit out on the point to watch the gulls fight off turkey vultures and bald eagles to safe-guard their treats. Kurt never did become a good fisherman, nor did anyone else in our family. Our good friends Scott Kulczycki and Jimmy Cosgrove are the only people I ever knew who could get a walleye out of Burntside Lake that was worth eating. I buy our fresh walleye at Zup's super-market, and it has a sticker on it that says *local*, which really could mean Canada, eh?

For tartar sauce

1 cup mayonnaise

3 tablespoons chopped dill pickles

2 teaspoons dill pickle juice

1 teaspoon lemon zest

2 teaspoons fresh lemon juice

salt and black pepper, to taste

2 dashes hot sauce (Tabasco)

1 teaspoon chopped pickled or fresh jalapeño, optional

For walleye

2 cups vegetable oil, for frying

2 cups yellow cornmeal

1 cup all-purpose flour

2 teaspoons paprika

2 teaspoons Old Bay seasoning

1 teaspoon onion powder

1 teaspoon kosher salt, plus more for serving

3 large eggs

4 walleye fillets

For tartar sauce

In a medium bowl, stir sauce ingredients together. Ideally, make the tartar sauce 30 minutes ahead to let the flavors meld.

For walleye

Heat oil to 375 degrees in a large cast iron pan on the grill or stove top. Heat oven to 250 degrees.

In a zip-top bag, combine the cornmeal and flour with the seasonings. In a mixing bowl, beat the eggs. Dip fish in egg mixture and then shake the fillets in the bag with the flour mixture. Shake off any excess flour.

Fry the fish pieces in batches until golden brown, about 3 minutes per side. Keep fried fish warm in the oven while frying the other pieces. Sprinkle with kosher salt and serve with tartar sauce.

Kurt's BBQ Ribs

Serves 6

Over the years, my husband, Kurt, has tried countless recipes for ribs. He likes them a little meatier and chewier than I do. Frankly, I don't mind my ribs boiled before grilling and fall-off-the-bone soft. We've settled on the following recipe because the ribs stay meaty and chewy, but when wrapped in foil they steam and become much more tender. The recipe is loosely based on the "3-2-1" technique for making ribs, but this version takes fewer hours and uses no liquids during the foil-wrapped stage. If I had my way, I would add some cider vinegar to the foil packet to make the ribs softer. But hey, marriage is a compromise, and these are Kurt's Ribs. (Go ahead and try the vinegar or apple cider — up to one cup per rack — if you want.)

¼ cup brown sugar

2 tablespoons ground mustard

2 tablespoons smoked paprika

1 tablespoon chili powder

1 tablespoon kosher salt

1 teaspoon garlic salt

1 teaspoon onion powder

1 teaspoon black pepper

1 teaspoon cayenne

½ teaspoon ground cinnamon

2 racks ribs (baby back ribs or spareribs; spareribs are meaty and cheaper), membrane removed (see tip)

¼ cup barbecue sauce, plus more for serving

Mix spice rub ingredients together. Place the rack of ribs on a rimmed baking sheet and rub both sides with the spice rub.

Heat grill to 275 degrees (see tip). Cook the ribs for 2 hours over indirect heat. Then wrap each rack in aluminum foil and bake on indirect heat for another hour. (Wrapping the ribs in foil steams the ribs, making them extra tender.) Unwrap ribs and brush each rack with 2 tablespoons of barbecue sauce. Cook on low, direct heat, bone side down for 20 minutes to lacquer the barbecue sauce.

Cut into individual bones and serve with your favorite barbecue sauce.

NOTE: For grilling, we use a three-burner Weber with just one burner on medium or high. You can put soaked wood chips over the one burner. To hold in the heat and smoke, we plug up the back vent of the closed lid with a crumpled strip of aluminum foil.

TIP: To remove and discard the membrane: Place the ribs so the curve, or the back of the rack, is facing up. Use a sharp knife to slice under the membrane on one end of the rack just above the bone. Use your fingers to peel back the membrane; discard membrane. Or buy from a butcher and have them do this step for you.

Salted Coffee Brownies

Serves 12

Chocolate and salt always go together, like peanut butter and jelly. These brownies are perfect for breakfast with a cup of hot coffee as you sit on the dock watching for ducks to swim by or for loons to pop up from fishing the depths of the lake.

1 cup (2 sticks) unsalted butter

5 ounces unsweetened chocolate

1 tablespoon finely ground espresso or coffee

2 cups granulated sugar

1 teaspoon vanilla extract

5 large eggs

1 cup all-purpose flour

½ teaspoon kosher salt

1 tablespoon chocolate salt (see tip; or use plain kosher salt)

Heat oven to 350 degrees and grease a 9x13–inch baking pan.

In a heavy saucepan over low heat, melt the butter and chocolate with espresso or coffee, whisking until smooth. Remove from heat and cool for 10 minutes. Whisk in sugar and vanilla. Whisk in eggs, 1 at a time, until the mixture is glossy and smooth.

In a medium bowl, whisk together the flour and salt, then whisk dry mixture into the chocolate mixture. Spread the batter in the prepared pan and evenly sprinkle a layer of chocolate salt on top. Bake for 25–30 minutes. Cool for at least 30 minutes, then cut into squares.

TIP: Find chocolate salt at Golden Fig Fine Foods in St. Paul, Minnesota, or online at goldenfig.com.

No-Bake Layered Lemon Loaf with Blueberries

Serves 8

The town of Ely has an epic small-town Fourth of July parade. Each year we line up on Main Street and watch the different participants pass by. The Ely Clown Band is a favorite. So are the local kids on decorated bikes. A few politicians show up, plus the pro-mining folks and the "Save the Boundary Waters" folks, all vying for attention by seeing who can throw out the most candy. After the parade, we start the Fourth of July meal, usually with many of our friends. Ribs (page 118) and potato salad (page 110) with baked beans (page 35) are typically on the menu, but desserts vary depending on who attends. One year I saw a recipe in a magazine for a no-bake cake layered with cream cheese and graham crackers. It was a sweltering July, so I set out to make my version, grateful not to need the oven for it. This dessert was so delicious that every year after, on the Fourth of July, I make it again.

For lemon curd

zest of 3 lemons

¾ cup fresh lemon juice (from about 3 lemons)

1⅓ cups granulated sugar

5 large eggs

pinch kosher salt

¾ cup (1½ sticks) unsalted butter, cut into 1-inch pieces

For loaf

1½ cups mascarpone cheese

¾ cup heavy cream

¼ cup sour cream

20 graham crackers

1 pint blueberries, plus more for serving

For lemon curd

In a medium saucepan, whisk together the lemon zest, lemon juice, sugar, eggs, and salt. Heat the saucepan over medium heat. Cook, whisking constantly, until the mixture has thickened, about 15 minutes. Remove from the heat and whisk in the butter, 3 pats at a time, until fully incorporated and the mixture has a silky texture. Chill to room temperature or about 30 minutes, then continue with the recipe.

For loaf

Line a 9x5–inch loaf pan with plastic wrap, allowing 4 inches of extra plastic to hang over on each side.

In a large bowl, beat the mascarpone, heavy cream, and sour cream with an electric mixer until incorporated and smooth. With a spatula or a spoon, gently fold in 1 cup of cooled lemon curd (the extra curd is for snacking).

Spread approximately ⅔ cup of the lemon-cream mixture on the bottom of the pan, making about a ¼-inch layer. Place a single layer of graham crackers on top of the lemon-cream mixture, arranging to fit. Add another ⅔ cup lemon-cream mixture and then a layer of blueberries, about 1 cup. Repeat the layering process, ending with a final layer of lemon cream. Cover the cake by folding the layers of plastic wrap over the top.

Refrigerate 8 hours or overnight, until firm, so loaf will hold up on its own when sliced. Uncover the cake and invert onto a platter. Serve with blueberries on the side.

Blueberry Galette

Serves 8

Galettes are fashionable these days. The whole "rustic tart" thing is very Instagrammable. My husband, Kurt, used to make these free-form pies on the island with whatever fresh blueberries we could pick. Sometimes the galette was small because we had only two cups of berries, and sometimes they were much larger. This is one of the charms of the galette: make do with what you have. We didn't have a pie pan back in the day, so Kurt improvised. And back then, we didn't know what a galette was; we didn't know how trendsetting we were (insert laugh here). I *do* like rustic, though, and I think the galette, with its long curving crust that gets crispy and dark brown, looks fabulous on the table. Galettes are also delicious in the morning. A portion holds up enough so you can eat it like a slice of pizza with a cup of coffee standing over the butcher block counter when no one is looking. If you can find high-fat European butter, like Kerrygold, your crust will thank you. If not, a stick of unsalted butter works just fine.

For crust

1¼ cups all-purpose flour

½ teaspoon kosher salt

½ cup (1 stick) unsalted butter, chilled, cut into ½-inch cubes

3 tablespoons ice water

1 tablespoon vodka

For filling

3 cups blueberries

¼ cup plus 1 tablespoon granulated sugar

1 tablespoon cornstarch

1 teaspoon lemon zest

2 teaspoons fresh lemon juice

1 large egg

1 tablespoon water

For crust

Add flour and salt to a food processor. Pulse 2 to 3 times to combine. Scatter butter cubes over flour and pulse 4 to 5 times, until flour is evenly distributed. The dough should look crumbly. Add 3 tablespoons ice water through the tube, pulsing once each time. The crumbs should begin to form larger clusters. Add the vodka and continue to pulse until the dough comes together in a ball and awkwardly spins in the machine.

Remove dough from bowl and place in a mound on a clean surface. Work the dough just enough to form a ball. Flatten to a disk, wrap in plastic wrap, and refrigerate for at least 1 hour.

To assemble

Heat oven to 425 degrees and set the rack in the middle of the oven. Line a baking sheet with parchment. In a large bowl, toss together the blueberries, ¼ cup sugar, cornstarch, lemon zest, and lemon juice.

On a floured surface, roll dough ball into a circle ⅛ inch thick. Dust off any extra flour and lay the dough on the prepared sheet. Mound the blueberry filling in the middle of the crust. Fold and crimp the dough over the filling to cover at least 2 inches of the filling along the sides.

Just before baking, beat together the egg and 1 tablespoon water to form an egg wash. Brush the edges of the crust with egg wash. Dust the crust with the remaining 1 tablespoon of sugar. Bake for 30 minutes, then reduce heat to 375 degrees and bake for an additional 30 minutes.

Let cool for 30 minutes to allow galette to set. Serve warm.

WEDDING STORY

The tornado that missed us in the late seventies cut a neat alley down the middle of both Brownell and Miller Islands. By the nineties, the trees were all gone, decomposed into the contour of the rocks, allowing the berry bushes to grow wild — prime spots for picking blueberries and raspberries. Miller Island was private, with cabin owners we didn't know, but Brownell had just the ruins of an old cabin from the 1920s, built by a local lumberman, Jim Brownell. Each summer he'd throw a party with a group of other lumber barons, mine owners, and managers called the Sunshine Boys Club. They'd bring out huge quantities of fresh fish, lobsters, clams, and oysters, freighted in from the East Coast, and have a big, boozy party on the island. What remains there now is just the brick foundation of the cabin as well as empty beer and whiskey bottles, and if you look through the overgrown woods closely, you can still find oyster shells. Brownell Island was our secret blueberry picking spot.

The day Kurt asked me to marry him we'd picked enough raspberries and blueberries to make a bumbleberry pie. For dinner that evening we planned beer-can chicken and fresh corn on the cob. I rubbed the chicken with a mix of spices like paprika, cayenne, dried thyme, and salt. Kurt heated the grill to 300 degrees, drank a can of beer, then filled the can back up with water (there is no need to waste actual beer when making beer-can chicken; the can simply stands the bird upright; see page 84). We put the chicken on the grill on indirect heat, closed the hood, and headed out in the boat for a happy hour cocktail cruise. Kurt drove the Lund over to Miller Island.

On the back of Miller Island, a pair of bald eagles had built a nest high in an old-growth white pine just after the tornado carved its alley. Over the years we'd seen half a dozen or more eagle chicks being raised into juveniles. Kurt drove the boat slowly around Miller Island and then cut the motor in front of the nest. I was looking through the binoculars to spot the eagles when he got down on his knee. At the time I thought he was just bending over to tie his shoe, but then he pulled a ring case from his pocket and opened it. *Will you marry me?*

I cried. We'd been living together for five years, and I expected to be asked at some point, but marriage was not something I felt like I needed to do just then. It seemed like marriage would come sometime down the road when we wanted to have kids or buy a house together or open a joint checking account. I really had no idea he'd ask, and I was taken aback, shocked, and happily surprised. I said, "Are you sure you want to?" He said, "Yes, so . . . what do you say?" I said, "Yes." And only then did he pull from the glove box two cut crystal flutes and a bottle of Perrier-Jouët champagne with its anemone flower–wreathed label.

We married the following June and took a two-week honeymoon. The first week we spent at a small beach town in Oaxaca, Mexico, called Puerto Escondido. We stayed at the only resort hotel there, the Hotel Santa Fe. Aside from the locals, the town was filled with surfers from all over the world who came to surf the "Mexican Pipeline." The monster waves on this beach were over twenty feet high, and those kids would go out every morning to get crushed. We'd have our *café con leche* and fabulous sugar-coated pastries while we watched the surfing carnage. In the evening we ate avocados with salt, fresh corn tortillas, and, among other things, fresh-caught red snapper grilled whole with olive oil, garlic, and salt.

The second week of our honeymoon we spent on True North Island. It rained the whole time. This is always the quandary: what do you do in the summer on an island when it rains all day? Kurt has almost no tolerance for puzzles or board games, there's no TV to watch, twenty-five years ago there was no internet or social media to scroll through, and even the usual honeymoon activities get old after a while. We cooked stews, soups, chili, and pan-fried meat. We made big breakfasts of bacon, eggs, hash browns, and also my Dutch Baby Pancake (page 56). We went into town for some meals just to get out of the cabin, and we did some of the tourist things we typically didn't have time for. We saw the wolves and pups at the International Wolf Center in Ely, and we drove to Tower and did the Soudan Underground Mine Tour, where retired miners take you deep down the shaft in the old freight elevator, put you in the original ore cars, and give a tour through the tunnels. If you come to Ely, I highly recommend the Soudan Mine.

Kurt and I have been married for more than twenty-five years. On the island we celebrate each anniversary with a quiet dinner, flowers, and the acknowledgment that since we've gotten this far, we can probably go the distance. We celebrate my birthday each Memorial Day not so quietly, with friends and family gathered to drink cocktails, open gifts, and have a huge dinner party out on the deck (weather permitting, of course). Most years we grill butterflied leg of lamb marinated in olive oil, salt, pepper, garlic, and rosemary, served with couscous and fresh asparagus. Last year my niece Skyler and I made a white cake with whipped cream frosting and topped it with strawberries. Two years ago, Dominic proposed to my niece Anna on the lake. Maybe one day my daughter, Ellie? The cycle continues . . .

Spicy Cilantro Moscow Mule

Serves 1

When I entertain, I put out a classic bar setup with vodka, gin, whiskey, wine, beer, and mixers. I also try to have a signature cocktail for the evening, something the guests usually wouldn't make at home. This recipe takes the traditional Moscow mule up a notch and starts the evening off in a festive way.

1 tablespoon chopped cilantro, plus sprig for garnish

1 ounce fresh lime juice

2 jalapeño slices, seeded

2 ounces vodka

4 ounces ginger beer

Muddle the chopped cilantro, lime juice, and 1 jalapeño slice in a copper mug. Fill the mug with ice, pour in vodka and ginger beer, and stir. Garnish with a sprig of cilantro and the remaining jalapeño slice.

Cucumber-Jalapeño Margarita

Serves 1

This margarita builds upon Lila's Simply Perfect Margarita (page 53), which is a basic recipe. This version uses fresh cucumbers and jalapeños, which are abundant in our Hilltop Garden in late July and August.

3 slices jalapeño, with seeds

3 slices cucumber

2 lime wedges

2 ounces silver tequila

2 ounces Cointreau or simple syrup

2 ounces fresh lime juice

kosher salt

Muddle the jalapeños, 2 slices cucumber, and 1 lime wedge in a cocktail shaker. Fill the shaker with ice, and add the tequila, Cointreau or simple syrup, and lime juice. Cover and shake to combine all ingredients.

Run the edge of a lime wedge around the rim of a rocks glass. Dip the rim of the glass in kosher salt. Add ice. Strain the contents of the shaker into the ice-filled glass. Garnish with the lime wedge and remaining cucumber slice.

Cucumber Vinegar Salad

Serves 6

We love this salad in the summer, and it's *sooo* fast and easy to prepare. It also uses up plenty of Hilltop Garden cucumbers when they're abundant. My husband, Kurt, remembers his grandmother making this salad out on the farm in Nebraska when he was a child, and it's still one of his favorites. It's nice to serve on a hot day alongside fried chicken or walleye. Leftovers of this salad keep well in the refrigerator and are great for lunch with some pita, hummus, olives, and chunks of feta, all drizzled with olive oil and honey.

3 cucumbers peeled, halved, seeded, thinly sliced into half moons

½ cup sliced onions (Vidalia preferred, but any will do)

1 tablespoon kosher salt

1 cup plus 2 tablespoons water

½ cup distilled white vinegar

½ cup granulated sugar

¼ cup chopped fresh dill

Place cucumbers and onions in a bowl. Add salt and 1 cup water. Weigh them down (for example, with an unopened can of crushed tomatoes) to soak in the brine for 2–4 hours. Drain and rinse off excess salt with cold water. Lightly squeeze the cucumbers by hand to extract moisture.

In a separate bowl, mix 2 tablespoons water, vinegar, and sugar until sugar is dissolved. Pour mixture over cucumbers. Add dill before serving.

Roasted Beet Salad with Blueberries and Balsamic Dressing

Serves 4

Some salads speak to specific decades. The eighties, for me, were Asian salads with mandarin oranges and crispy wontons (which I still love). The nineties were Caesar salads with chicken and mustard vinaigrette. The 2000s were beet salads with balsamic vinaigrette and fried goat cheese medallions à la Alice Waters at Chez Panisse in Berkeley, California. The 2020s are moving toward heartier steak salads, meals unto themselves, so I seem to be a decade or two behind here. No matter! This salad is heaven if you can time it to take advantage of fresh-picked blueberries. Store-bought berries will be fine, of course, but the super sweet fresh berries can't be *beet* (ha!).

For dressing
½ cup blueberries, mashed or muddled

¼ cup extra-virgin olive oil

2 tablespoons balsamic vinegar

2 tablespoons honey (or maple syrup)

1 tablespoon fresh lemon juice

pinch kosher salt

pinch black pepper

For salad
2 large or 3 medium beets, peeled and cut into 1-inch chunks

1 tablespoon extra-virgin olive oil

1 teaspoon kosher salt

6 cups spinach or spring mix lettuce

1 cup blueberries

1 cup crumbled feta cheese

1 cup roasted walnut pieces

For dressing
Shake all ingredients in a Mason jar or blend in a blender.

For salad
Heat oven to 400 degrees. On a rimmed baking sheet, toss beet chunks with olive oil and salt. Roast for 30 minutes. Set aside to cool.

Assemble salad by placing greens on a pretty platter or beautiful serving dish and arranging the blueberries and cooled beets on top, in rows or mounded in a pile. Sprinkle the salad with feta cheese and walnuts. Drizzle with dressing.

Chunky Greek Salad with Croutons

Serves 6

For croutons

3 cups stale bread cut into 1-inch cubes

1 tablespoon extra-virgin olive oil

1 teaspoon dried oregano

For dressing

½ cup extra-virgin olive oil

¼ cup red wine vinegar

1 tablespoon fresh lemon juice

1 clove garlic, minced or grated

1 teaspoon Dijon mustard

2 teaspoons dried oregano

1 teaspoon kosher salt

1 teaspoon black pepper

For salad

1 pint cherry tomatoes, halved

1 cucumber, seeded, chopped (if using a Persian cucumber, no need to remove the seeds)

½ cup pitted kalamata olives

⅓ cup thinly sliced red onion

1 (8-ounce) block feta cheese, cut into cubes

¼ cup chopped Italian flat-leaf parsley

1 tablespoon fresh oregano leaves, optional

For croutons

Heat oven to 350 degrees. Toss the bread cubes in olive oil with dried oregano. Dump cubes onto a rimmed baking sheet. Bake for 12–15 minutes or until crisp.

For dressing

Place ingredients in a large Mason jar and shake to combine.

For salad

Place the tomatoes, cucumbers, kalamata olives, red onions, and feta cheese in a large serving bowl. Toss the salad with the croutons and ⅓ cup dressing. Let sit 10 minutes to allow dressing to absorb. Toss again and taste before serving. Add more dressing if the salad seems dry. Sprinkle with parsley and fresh oregano (if using).

Lemony Zucchini Ribbon Salad

Serves 6

This salad is a surprise. You wouldn't think eating raw zucchini would be great, but when you shave fresh garden zucchini into delicate ribbons, it takes on a whole new personality. If you grow zucchini, you know that by mid-August the neighbors pretend they aren't home when they see you coming with your arms full. No matter how few plants I put in the ground, I always end up with too much zucchini. This salad can knock out a bunch I have sitting on the counter. Also, this recipe may save me a trip into town for more salad greens when I am out on the island.

2 tablespoons raw pine nuts

5 small zucchini, ends removed, sliced into ribbons with a vegetable peeler

1 teaspoon lemon zest

3 tablespoons fresh lemon juice

1 tablespoon extra-virgin olive oil

kosher salt and freshly ground black pepper, to taste

½ cup Parmesan cheese shaved with a vegetable peeler

1 tablespoon finely chopped fresh mint (or fresh basil, dill, or parsley)

Toast the pine nuts in a dry cast iron skillet over medium heat until they just start to get lightly brown, about 5 minutes.

In a large bowl, toss together the zucchini ribbons, lemon zest, lemon juice, and olive oil. Season with salt and pepper; taste and adjust seasoning, if desired. Arrange zucchini ribbons in a mound on a serving platter. Top with Parmesan cheese. Sprinkle salad with the toasted pine nuts and fresh herbs.

Garden Gazpacho

Serves 6-8

You're either a gazpacho person, or you're not — some people just don't dig cold soup. My mother-in-law, Dolores, was the first person to turn me on to the joy of cold soup (see also Ellie's Vichyssoise, page 62). We like to eat cold soup outside for lunch in August when the Hilltop Garden is generating fresh veggies, or when the Ely Tuesday night farmers' market in Whiteside Park is open and the locals are selling their produce (you can also buy hand-made crafts and jams and jellies, and lately a local wood-fired pizza truck has made an appearance).

6 medium garden tomatoes

½ cup chopped green bell pepper

½ cup chopped red onion

1 cucumber, peeled, seeded, cut into chunks

1 clove garlic

1 teaspoon chopped fresh dill, plus a few sprigs for garnish

⅓ cup extra-virgin olive oil

2 teaspoons white wine vinegar

2 teaspoons kosher salt

Add all ingredients to a blender. Blend for 1–2 minutes, until combined. Serve with fresh dill as a garnish.

Bacon, Corn, and Potato Chowder

Serves 4-6

I love soup. I always have a stock bag in the freezer at the cabin with vegetable scraps, dried onion skins, and chicken parts and bones. When the bag gets full, I add water and salt and boil on the stove until I get a rich stock. I also save the cobs from the ears of corn I use in this recipe to enrich the chicken stock base of this chowder. Everyone likes bacon, corn, and potatoes, and when you add a loaf of crusty sourdough bread and a green salad, you have a cozy, rainy-night-with-a-north-wind cabin meal.

3 tablespoons butter, divided

8 slices bacon, chopped

2 cloves garlic, chopped

1 medium onion, finely chopped

¼ cup all-purpose flour

6 cups chicken broth

2 large Yukon Gold potatoes, cut into 1-inch pieces

leaves from 6 sprigs fresh thyme

1 bay leaf

6 cups corn cut off the cob (about 4 large ears of corn), cobs reserved

1 cup sliced green onions, both white and light green parts

2 cups (1 pint) heavy cream

2 teaspoons kosher salt

2 teaspoons freshly ground black pepper

Place 1 tablespoon butter in a large pot over medium-high heat. Add chopped bacon and cook until browned. Use a slotted spoon to transfer bacon to a paper towel to drain. To the same pot, add remaining 2 tablespoons butter, garlic, and onions. Cook for about 3 minutes, until onions are translucent. Sprinkle flour over the onion mixture and cook, stirring, for 1 minute. Add broth, potatoes, thyme, and bay leaf, stirring to combine. Add the reserved corn cobs. Simmer for 25 minutes uncovered, then remove corn cobs and bay leaf. Add corn, bacon, green onions, and heavy cream to the pot. Continue cooking for about 5 minutes, adding salt and pepper to taste.

Anna's Burntside Dip

Serves 4-6

The Leer family is close-knit. Charlie is the oldest, followed by Christopher, Anna, and Grace. Kristi is their mom and my sister-in-law. Everyone lives in California now but comes out to Burntside Lake each summer. The kids have fond memories of campfires and s'mores at the point and fishing off the dock. Over time, everyone has started to request their favorite dishes year after year, and Anna's appetizer dip is a perennial pick. It gets served in the eggplant-shaped Le Creuset dish that Kristi found at the thrift store in town for three dollars.

½ cup extra-virgin olive oil

2 garlic scapes, thinly sliced (or substitute 1 garlic clove, minced or grated)

2 green onions, white and light green parts, thinly sliced

1 teaspoon crushed red pepper

2 tablespoons finely chopped cilantro (leaves and stems), plus more for garnish

2 cups plain unsweetened Greek yogurt

½ cup sour cream

2 teaspoons lemon zest

3 tablespoons fresh lemon juice

1 teaspoon kosher salt

10 grinds freshly cracked black pepper

crackers, baguette slices, or vegetables, for serving

Heat the olive oil, garlic scapes, green onions, crushed red pepper, and cilantro in a small cast iron skillet over medium-low heat. Cook, swirling occasionally, until the scapes and green onions start to sizzle and frizzle and the crushed red pepper turns the oil bright orange. Remove from the heat and allow to cool.

In a medium bowl, combine the yogurt, sour cream, lemon zest, and lemon juice. Season with salt and pepper. Spoon into a serving bowl and swirl in the sizzled garlic scape/scallion oil mixture. Garnish with cilantro stems.

Serve with crackers, baguette slices, or vegetables.

Baked Zucchini Fries with Lemon Aioli

Serves 4

In the quest for more zucchini ideas during the plentiful season, I stumbled upon zucchini fries. Don't get me wrong — these are not a replacement for french fries. But when you have eight zucchini staring you in the face and three people at the table, this is a great idea. The zucchini are baked, not fried, so you won't be standing at the stove in your bathing suit and getting your stomach burned with spattering oil (which may or may not have happened one summer).

For aioli

¾ cup mayonnaise

¼ cup sour cream

zest of 1 lemon (about 2 teaspoons)

1 tablespoon lemon juice

1 large clove garlic, minced or grated

1 teaspoon kosher salt

For fries

⅓ cup all-purpose flour

2 large eggs plus 1 large egg white

1 tablespoon water

1 cup panko bread crumbs

½ cup grated Parmesan cheese

2 teaspoons chopped fresh rosemary leaves

1 teaspoon kosher salt

½ teaspoon black pepper

2 medium zucchini, cut into ½-inch by 4-inch batons

For aioli

Combine all ingredients in a bowl about 30 minutes before serving to let the flavors meld.

For fries

Heat oven to 425 degrees. Line a baking sheet with paper towels or newspaper for serving.

Place flour in a shallow dish. Whisk eggs, egg white, and water in another shallow dish until foamy. Combine bread crumbs, Parmesan cheese, rosemary, salt, and pepper in a third shallow dish.

Working in batches, toss zucchini in flour to coat. Then dip into the egg mixture, shaking off the excess. Finally, toss in the bread crumb mixture, pressing to adhere. Place on a baking sheet while you finish the batch.

Bake without touching for 10 minutes. Flip and bake for 10 more minutes. Slide fries onto prepared baking sheet and serve.

Sesame-Crusted Pork Loin

137

August

Serves 4

I think pork loin is generally the most overrated cut of meat there is. It has certainly succeeded in being "The Other White Meat" — just as dry and flavorless as chicken breasts. But mother-in-law Dolores's sesame-crusted pork loin changed my feelings. The marinated meat retains a salty, citrusy flavor, and the crunchy nuttiness of the sesame seeds turns the pork loin from ho-hum to oh-yum. We serve this with plain rice, or fried rice if we have bits of veggies floating around that we need to use up, along with Sesame Sugar Snap Peas (page 138). We plant peas in the Hilltop Garden and usually get enough to make this meal a few times throughout the summer.

¼ cup soy sauce

2 tablespoons peanut butter

2 tablespoons molasses

1 tablespoon brown sugar

2 teaspoons rice wine vinegar

2 teaspoons sesame oil

1 teaspoon hot sauce (Tabasco)

1 teaspoon honey

1 clove garlic, minced

pinch black pepper

1 (16-ounce) pork tenderloin

3 tablespoons sesame seeds

Mix soy sauce, peanut butter, molasses, brown sugar, rice wine vinegar, sesame oil, hot sauce, honey, garlic, and pepper in a zip-top bag. Add pork tenderloin and marinate in the refrigerator for at least 6 hours and up to 24 hours.

Heat grill to 425 degrees. Discard marinade. Scatter the sesame seeds on a plate and roll the marinated pork tenderloin in the sesame seeds. Grill on indirect heat for 15 minutes or until a meat thermometer reads 145 degrees. Allow to rest for 5 minutes before serving.

Sesame Sugar Snap Peas

Serves 4

These usually get served with Sesame-Crusted Pork Loin (page 137) when the peas are fresh from the Ely Hilltop Garden.

2 teaspoons toasted sesame oil

1 teaspoon chili oil crunch (available at grocery stores; or substitute a pinch of crushed red pepper)

3 cups sugar snap peas, trimmed

1 tablespoon sesame seeds

1 teaspoon soy sauce

Heat sesame oil and chili oil in a cast iron skillet over medium-high heat until the oil shimmers. Add snap peas and stir until they turn bright green and start to become tender, about 4 minutes. Sprinkle sesame seeds over the peas and stir a few times to mix. Add soy sauce, toss, and serve.

Summer Corn Risotto

Serves 4

I love making this dish in the summer, but I also re-create it at home in the winter with corn I've frozen in two-cup portions. I usually freeze ten to twelve zip-top bags of sweet corn to get me through the year, so I always have the ingredients for corn risotto and Bacon, Corn, and Potato Chowder (page 134) on hand. The trick is to freeze the kernels on a rimmed baking sheet first so they don't all clump together in a big frozen brick. Corn freezes beautifully and still tastes summer sweet when cooked.

5 cups chicken broth

2 tablespoons butter

2 cups sweet corn (from 2 large or 3 small ears of corn)

1 teaspoon kosher salt

1 teaspoon black pepper

1 tablespoon extra-virgin olive oil

1 cup finely chopped onion

3 cloves garlic, minced

1½ cups arborio rice

⅓ cup freshly grated Parmesan cheese

2 tablespoons fresh herbs (basil, dill, cilantro, parsley, oregano, or chives)

In a saucepan, bring chicken broth to a boil, then turn the heat to low to keep warm.

In a medium cast iron pan over medium heat, melt butter, then add sweet corn and cook, stirring, until corn is cooked through, about 4 minutes. Stir in salt and pepper and set aside.

In a medium saucepan over medium heat, add olive oil and onions and cook, stirring, until starting to turn tender, 2 minutes. Add garlic and cook 1 minute more. Add rice, stirring for another minute. Add 1 cup chicken broth, stirring until nearly absorbed, then add additional broth 1 cup at a time, stirring until rice is creamy and al dente, 25–30 minutes total cooking time (when the rice becomes creamy, add more broth depending on desired consistency).

Remove from heat and stir in corn and Parmesan cheese, then sprinkle with fresh herbs before serving.

Cavatappi Pasta Salad with Basil Pesto

Serves 8

Cavatappi pasta (long, squiggly tubes) is a fun shape for this salad, but you can also substitute rotini, penne, conchiglie, or a dozen others. The key to this recipe is the fresh basil and garden cherry tomatoes that take a simple salad and make it taste like the ambrosia that is the summer garden. My daughter, Ellie, used to eat so much pesto that my mom joked that the kid always smelled like garlic. I know it was true.

For pesto
2 cups fresh basil leaves

½ cup raw walnuts

1 tablespoon lemon zest

2 tablespoons fresh lemon juice

3 small cloves garlic

⅓ cup extra-virgin olive oil

½ teaspoon kosher salt

freshly ground black pepper

For salad
1 (16-ounce) box cavatappi pasta, cooked according to package directions, drained and rinsed

2 tablespoons extra-virgin olive oil

3 cups cherry tomatoes, halved

1 teaspoon kosher salt

1 tablespoon lemon zest

1 tablespoon fresh lemon juice

½ cup grated Parmesan cheese

For pesto
Pulse the basil, nuts, lemon zest, lemon juice, and garlic in a food processor until finely chopped. With the blade running, drizzle the olive oil through the tube. Stop the processor, add salt and pepper, give another pulse, and taste. Adjust seasonings to your liking.

For salad
Toss pasta with olive oil. Add pesto and cherry tomatoes, salt, lemon zest, and lemon juice, and toss to coat the pasta. Add Parmesan cheese and toss again before serving.

VARIATIONS

Use cilantro, parsley, or mint (or any combination of the herbs) in place of basil.

Try pine nuts or almonds in place of the walnuts.

Use mini mozzarella balls or chunks of feta in addition to or instead of Parmesan cheese.

Add blanched broccoli florets or sliced pepperoni.

Add Greek olives.

Blackened Green Beans

Serves 4

I first tried these at a friend's farmhouse in the small community of Embarrass, Minnesota. The beans were harvested from the extensive kitchen garden and cooked outside on a large, twenty-inch cast-iron skillet big enough to deep-fry two cut-up chickens. The reason you might want to cook this outside on a grill is that the spiced and coated beans added to a 500-degree skillet yields a toxic plume of smoke that in an enclosed space makes your eyes water and sends you into a coughing fit. On our three-burner grill with the lid closed, I can get the skillet hot enough in about twenty minutes. After a few minutes of cooking, the blackened beans will still have a slight crunch and carry that hot, charred taste. Always great with a nice ribeye.

3 cups green beans, ends trimmed

1 teaspoon extra-virgin olive oil

2 tablespoons paprika

1 teaspoon cayenne

1 teaspoon chili powder

1 teaspoon garlic powder

1 teaspoon ground cumin

2 teaspoons kosher salt

2 tablespoons butter

In a medium bowl, toss beans and olive oil. In a small bowl, thoroughly mix spices and salt. Add spices to green beans and toss to combine.

Heat a large, dry cast iron pan to almost smoking on the grill using direct heat — aim for 450–500 degrees. Add butter and green beans to the skillet and cook undisturbed until beans begin to blacken, approximately 2 minutes. Shake pan to redistribute beans and let cook for 1 minute more. Some beans will be blackened, and some may shrivel. Serve hot.

Green Bean, Potato, and Parsley Pesto Salad

Serves 8

This salad is another summer stunner with the starchy potatoes giving a little heft to the green beans and fresh herbs. Serve this alongside any of your favorite grilled meats or as a light summer meal with a cheese and spread platter and a side of crusty bread. This salad can be served cold, hot, or at room temperature. It holds up very well, so it's nice to make in advance for a potluck or party, or as a side dish for a picnic served on a long, adventurous pontoon ride.

For pesto

- **1½ cups parsley leaves and stems, roughly chopped**
- **1 cup basil leaves**
- **½ cup raw pine nuts**
- **1 tablespoon lemon zest**
- **2 tablespoons lemon juice**
- **3 small cloves garlic**
- **½ cup extra-virgin olive oil**
- **½ teaspoon kosher salt**
- **freshly ground black pepper**

For salad

- **8 small red potatoes, halved or quartered (if large)**
- **1 pound green beans, trimmed, halved (about 35–40 beans)**
- **1 teaspoon kosher salt**
- **2 teaspoons lemon zest**
- **¼ cup grated Parmesan cheese**
- **freshly cracked black pepper**

For pesto

Pulse the parsley, basil, nuts, lemon zest, lemon juice, and garlic in a food processor until finely chopped. With the blade running, drizzle the olive oil through the tube until consistency is smooth. Finish with salt and pepper to taste.

For salad

Boil potatoes until tender and easily pierced with a knife, about 20 minutes. About 5 minutes before potatoes are done, add beans and cook until tender but still crisp or al dente. Drain potatoes and beans and rinse under cold water.

In a bowl, gently toss the potatoes and green beans with 1 cup pesto. Try not to break up the potatoes too much. Add salt, lemon zest, Parmesan cheese, and black pepper to taste and give salad a final toss.

Mississippi Roast à la Burntside with Creamy Horseradish Sauce

Serves 8

The first time I had this roast was at stepmom Kathy's house in Wisconsin. It was hard to believe the brine of pepperoncini could tenderize a pot roast and make the meat so delicious. I've experimented with pickles, but I keep coming back to the original. This recipe calls for the roast to be cooked in the oven, but you could also use a slow cooker: cook the meat on low for six hours.

For sauce

6 tablespoons prepared horseradish

¼ cup sour cream

¼ cup plain unsweetened Greek yogurt

1 tablespoon mayonnaise

1 teaspoon Dijon mustard

1 teaspoon fresh lemon juice

½ teaspoon kosher salt

For roast

1 tablespoon extra-virgin olive oil

1 (4-pound) boneless chuck roast

¼ cup chopped fresh parsley

2 tablespoons garlic powder

1 tablespoon dried dill

1 tablespoon kosher salt

1 teaspoon black pepper

4 tablespoons butter, cut into chunks

1 (16-ounce) jar pepperoncini, brine reserved

1 (10.5-ounce) can beef consommé

mashed potatoes or buns

sliced red onions

For sauce

Mix ingredients together. Serve as a sauce for the roast or as a spread for sandwiches.

For roast

Heat oven to 350 degrees. Heat oil in a Dutch oven over medium-high heat. Brown the roast, about 3 minutes per side. Sprinkle parsley, garlic powder, dill, salt, and pepper on the roast. Place chunks of butter on top of the roast. Arrange the pepperoncini all around the roast and pour in the brine and beef consommé. Cover the pan with foil and fit the lid tightly on top of the foil. Bake for 3 hours. The roast is done when it is fall-apart tender and can be shredded with a fork.

Serve on mashed potatoes or on buns with sliced red onion and creamy horseradish sauce on the side.

Grilled Ratatouille with Herb Vinaigrette

Serves 6

Ratatouille is one of my favorite sides for any cut of lamb. This French Provençal dish uses end-of-season vegetables that may be turning fleshy and overripe. The recipe starts with the vegetables cooked on the grill, which provides a great charred flavor. If I'm overwhelmed with vegetables from my garden late in August, I cook up a triple or quadruple batch and freeze in pint-size Mason jars. Later in the year, I use the thawed ratatouille in pasta, risotto, or tapenade for crostini.

For vinaigrette

1 tablespoon fresh lemon juice

1 tablespoon extra-virgin olive oil

1 tablespoon minced or grated garlic

1 tablespoon finely chopped fresh basil leaves

2 teaspoons finely chopped Italian flat-leaf parsley

1 teaspoon finely chopped fresh thyme leaves

For ratatouille

4 Roma tomatoes, halved lengthwise

2 medium zucchini, quartered lengthwise

1 large yellow squash, quartered lengthwise

2 medium Japanese eggplants (or substitute 1 globe eggplant), quartered lengthwise

1 large yellow onion, cut into ½-inch rounds

1 red bell pepper, halved, seeded

1 yellow bell pepper, halved, seeded

¼ cup extra-virgin olive oil

kosher salt and freshly ground black pepper

leaves from 8 sprigs fresh thyme

For vinaigrette

Add vinaigrette ingredients to a Mason jar and shake to combine.

For ratatouille

Place vegetables faceup on a rimmed baking sheet and drizzle with oil, salt, pepper, and fresh thyme. Toss with your hands to coat. Grill until blistered and browned, about 3 minutes per side for zucchini, squash, and tomatoes and about 5 minutes per side for eggplant, onion, and peppers.

Transfer vegetables and any juices to a bowl. Toss vegetables with the herb vinaigrette. Add salt to taste and a few grinds of fresh black pepper.

Anna and Dominic's Family Bolognese

Serves 6-8

This recipe is a cozy family favorite for the Leones. Anna was a Leer before she became a Leone by marrying Dominic, who proposed during a canoe trip on Burntside Lake. The Leer/Leones love to gather the extended clan around the Ely table and serve this family-style. Everyone loves a hearty Bolognese. This recipe is best paired with warm, crusty garlic bread and your favorite red wine.

¼ cup extra-virgin olive oil

1 medium yellow onion, chopped

4 cloves garlic, chopped

1 rib celery, chopped

1 carrot, chopped

1 pound ground beef

1 (28-ounce) can crushed tomatoes

¼ cup chopped Italian flat-leaf parsley

10 fresh basil leaves, chopped

1 (16-ounce) box rigatoni pasta

salt and freshly ground black pepper

¼ cup freshly grated Pecorino Romano

Heat a large skillet over medium heat and add the olive oil. Add the onions and garlic and cook, stirring, until the onions become soft and translucent, about 7 minutes. Add the celery and carrot and cook, stirring, for 5 more minutes. Increase the heat to high and add the ground beef, using a spoon to break up any large chunks. Cook for about 10 minutes, until no longer pink. Reduce heat to medium-low and add the crushed tomatoes, parsley, and basil. Cook until the sauce reduces and thickens, about 30 minutes.

Meanwhile, cook pasta according to package instructions until al dente; drain and return to pasta pot. Season sauce with salt and pepper and finish with Pecorino Romano cheese. Add Bolognese to pasta and give it a good toss. Serve it up in a large bowl.

Charlie and Melissa's Grilled Burntside Chicken Thighs

Serves 6

All the Leer kids live in California. Charlie is the oldest and Kurt's godson. Charlie has always loved fishing on the dock at Burntside, and he brings his wife, Melissa, back to the lake each summer to do just that. When Melissa was pregnant with their first child, he bought a pink child's fishing pole to pass on the tradition of catching bass off the dock. Charlie and Melissa prepared this dish in the summer of 2020 for their turn cooking for Grandma Dolores, and she gave it rave reviews.

Serve with Red Mexican Rice (page 147), Green Tomato Salsa Verde (page 148), and Corn off the Cob Elote Style (page 149).

½ cup extra-virgin olive oil

3 tablespoons brown sugar

3 tablespoons soy sauce

3 tablespoons chopped cilantro

1 teaspoon lime zest

1 tablespoon fresh lime juice

1½ teaspoons minced garlic

1 teaspoon kosher salt

½ teaspoon black pepper

6 bone-in, skin-on chicken thighs

Whisk olive oil, brown sugar, soy sauce, cilantro, lime zest, lime juice, garlic, salt, and pepper in a zip-top bag. Add chicken thighs and marinate in the refrigerator for at least 1 hour.

Heat grill to 350 degrees. Discard marinade. Grill thighs for 6 minutes per side or until internal temperature reaches 165 degrees.

Red Mexican Rice

Serves 6

This rice makes the perfect bed for serving Charlie and Melissa's Grilled Burntside Chicken Thighs (page 146).

3 tablespoons butter

2 cups long-grain white rice

¼ cup finely chopped onion

1 medium clove garlic, chopped

1 tablespoon ground cumin

1 teaspoon kosher salt

2 cups mild chunky salsa

1 cup chicken broth

¼ cup chopped green onions, green parts only

Melt butter in a medium saucepan over medium heat. Add rice, onions, garlic, cumin, and salt and cook, stirring, for 2 minutes. Add salsa and chicken broth to the pot and mix well. Turn the heat to low and cover. Simmer for 15 minutes or until liquid is absorbed and vent holes appear on the top of the rice. Transfer rice to a bowl and garnish with chopped green onions.

Green Tomato Salsa Verde

Makes about 2 cups

The first year we had the Hilltop Garden, we planted a ton of tomatoes right around Memorial Day. Ely is a Zone 3 garden climate, and I did not buy the kinds of tomatoes that would be ripe by the time we closed the cabin on Labor Day. After that, husband Kurt and I were headed out west on a campervan trip. So, at the end of the summer I had just a handful of red tomatoes and a slew of green ones, and if I didn't pick the green tomatoes, I wouldn't have much of a harvest at all. I did the best I could, fried just a few, and with most of the rest made quarts of green tomato salsa verde. If you find yourself with loads of green tomatoes, this recipe is an easy solution. Now I reserve some green tomatoes every year to get at least four to six pints of green tomato salsa verde. The pectin in the tomatoes can make the salsa super thick after canning, so feel free to add a little water, chicken stock, or lemon juice.

1 pound green tomatoes (about 6–8), halved

1 jalapeño, sliced lengthwise, seeded

2 cloves garlic, peeled

1 small white onion, quartered

½ cup cilantro leaves

3 tablespoons fresh lime juice

1 teaspoon kosher salt, or more to taste

Heat oven to broil. Line a baking sheet with foil. Lay tomatoes, jalapeño, garlic, and onions, cut side down, on the baking sheet. Roast for 15 minutes, or until the tomatoes, peppers, and onions start to brown and blister on top. Remove from the oven and let cool for 15 minutes.

Transfer the vegetables to a blender or food processor. Add the cilantro, lime juice, and salt, and pulse the mixture until it reaches the desired consistency.

TIPS: To make a chunky garden salsa, add ½ cup peeled and diced cucumber to the salsa verde. You can also add chopped fresh garden zucchini to the mixture.

Corn off the Cob Elote Style

Serves 4

One of my favorite Twin Cities Mexican restaurants is El Burrito Mercado. Milissa Silva along with her sisters are second-generation owners. Every weekend in the spring, summer, and fall, they sell elote at an outdoor stand at the back of the grocery store. My recipe is similar in flavor but uses corn cut off the cob. For kids with braces, don't ya know.

1 tablespoon butter

kernels cut from 4 ears of corn (about 4–5 cups)

2 tablespoons mayonnaise

¼ cup cotija cheese

1 tablespoon chopped Italian flat-leaf parsley

1 teaspoon smoked paprika

1 teaspoon kosher salt

freshly cracked black pepper, to taste

squeeze fresh lime juice

1 green onion, green part only, chopped

Melt butter in a large skillet over medium heat. Add corn and toss to coat. Spread the corn in an even layer and don't disturb it for 10–15 minutes, until it starts to char and blacken in some spots. Remove from heat and add mayonnaise, cotija cheese, parsley, paprika, salt, and pepper, tossing to combine. Serve on a platter or in a shallow bowl. Squeeze fresh lime juice on top and garnish with green onions.

Teriyaki Steak with Baked Rice

Serves 4

My mother-in-law, Dolores, made this for her family back in the sixties and seventies. It was one of Kurt's most memorable meals. It's now one of daughter Ellie's favorites, requested for her birthdays along with Kurt's Caesar Salad (page 17) and flourless Molten Chocolate Cakes (page 161). I'm not a big fan of sirloin steak — I think the cut lacks fat and flavor — so I typically cook it this way (that is, don't waste a good, expensive cut like ribeye or New York by using a marinade). I combined the steak recipe with the rice because they go together like butter and bread (it's just not the same with plain white rice or potatoes). Don't over-marinate the steak: it will start to break down and get mushy if left marinating for too long. Ellie always has me boil the marinade into a sauce to drizzle over her rice and steak.

For rice

2 tablespoons butter

½ cup chopped onion

1 cup long-grain white rice

2 cups chicken broth

For steak

½ cup soy sauce

¼ cup granulated sugar

3 cloves garlic, chopped

1 tablespoon ground ginger

1 teaspoon black pepper

1½ pounds top sirloin steak (¾ inch thick)

For rice

Heat oven to 375 degrees. Melt butter in a medium cast iron skillet. Add onions and cook, stirring, until translucent. Add the rice and cook 1 minute more, stirring to coat the grains of rice with the butter. Stir in chicken broth and let the mixture come to a boil. Cover and bake for 18 minutes.

For steak

In a shallow dish, combine soy sauce, sugar, garlic, ginger, and pepper. Add the steak and turn to coat. Cover and marinate for 2–3 hours.

Grill steak for 4 minutes on each side or until meat reaches desired doneness. Let meat rest before slicing.

In a saucepan, bring any leftover marinade to a boil for 5 minutes to create a sauce.

Serve sliced meat on a platter over rice and drizzled with sauce.

Zucchini Tart with Lemon Thyme Goat Cheese

Serves 8

This tart looks stunning on the table when zucchini slices are overlapped in concentric circles like a pinwheel. It's great served alongside a big green salad for a light summer supper or lunch. You can even wrap pieces in waxed paper or parchment and take them on a picnic.

For crust

1¼ cups all-purpose flour

½ cup (1 stick) unsalted butter, cold

1 teaspoon kosher salt

3 tablespoons ice water

1 tablespoon vodka

For filling

1½ pounds zucchini (about 3 medium), trimmed, cut into ⅛-inch rounds

2 teaspoons salt, plus more to taste

2 tablespoons extra-virgin olive oil, divided

4 ounces goat cheese, at room temperature

1¼ teaspoons chopped fresh lemon thyme leaves (or substitute regular thyme)

½ teaspoon lemon zest

freshly ground black pepper

For crust

In a food processor, pulse the flour, butter, and salt until the butter is the size of small peas. Add the ice water and vodka, 1 spoonful at a time, pulsing until the dough just comes together. Add 1 more tablespoon of water if needed. Flatten dough into a disk, wrap in plastic, and chill for 30 minutes.

On a well-floured surface or between sheets of parchment paper, roll the dough into an 11-inch round about ¼ inch thick. Place the dough on a baking sheet layered with parchment paper, cover with plastic wrap, and chill at least 30 minutes.

For filling

In a colander, toss the zucchini with salt and drain for 30 minutes. Gently squeeze the slices with your hands to release excess water, then transfer to a medium bowl. The slices should be more pliable.

Position a rack in the center of the oven and heat oven to 400 degrees. Toss the zucchini with 1 tablespoon olive oil. In a small bowl, mix the goat cheese with the lemon thyme, lemon zest, and salt and pepper to taste. Spread the cheese over the dough, leaving a ½-inch border around the outside. Arrange the zucchini rounds in tightly overlapping concentric circles all the way to the edge of the dough. (The rounds will shrink as they cook.) Drizzle with the remaining 1 tablespoon olive oil and bake for 40–50 minutes.

Ellie's Chocolate Zucchini Birthday Bundt Cake

Serves 10

My friend Zoë François, from the TV show *Zoë Bakes*, who makes everything beautiful, inspired this recipe. She convinced me I could put zucchini in Ellie's birthday cake without her knowing. While the ploy didn't work (I grated the zucchini too large on the box grater at the cabin, and flecks of green were visible), the cake was delicious nonetheless.

½ cup Dutch processed cocoa powder, plus ¼ cup for dusting the pan

¾ cup (1½ sticks) unsalted butter, softened

1 cup granulated sugar

⅓ cup packed brown sugar

3 large eggs

½ cup plain yogurt

¼ cup sour cream

1 teaspoon vanilla extract

2½ cups all-purpose flour

2 teaspoons baking powder

1 teaspoon baking soda

1 teaspoon kosher salt

1 teaspoon ground cinnamon

3 cups finely shredded zucchini (from about 4 medium zucchini), squeezed in a kitchen towel to extract all moisture (see tip)

strawberries and whipped cream, for serving

Heat oven to 350 degrees. Generously grease a Bundt pan and dust with ¼ cup cocoa powder to coat.

Beat the butter, granulated sugar, and brown sugar until creamy. Add the eggs, yogurt, sour cream, and vanilla, and beat again.

In a separate bowl, stir together the flour, remaining ½ cup cocoa powder, baking powder, baking soda, salt, and cinnamon. Gradually mix the dry ingredients with the wet ingredients until everything is incorporated. Stir in the zucchini by hand.

Pour batter into the prepared pan. Bake for 50–60 minutes, until a toothpick or knife inserted into the center of the cake comes out mostly clean. Cool cake in the pan for 15 minutes, then carefully flip it onto a plate and cool completely.

Serve with fresh strawberries and whipped cream.

TIP: Prepare the zucchini using a box grater or preferably the grater in a food processor so the shreds are smaller, thus hiding the green parts from young children.

Lemony Zucchini Bread

Serves 10

This bread is wonderful. Spread it with butter, cream cheese, or goat cheese for a lovely late-afternoon snack or breakfast tea bread. This bread freezes beautifully, and you can use the same recipe for muffins or mini loaves.

2 teaspoons lemon zest

½ cup plus 2 tablespoons granulated sugar, divided

2¼ cups zucchini grated on the large holes of a box grater

⅓ cup extra-virgin olive oil

5 tablespoons butter, melted and cooled

2 large eggs

½ cup packed brown sugar

1 teaspoon vanilla extract

1 teaspoon fresh lemon juice

2¼ cups all-purpose flour

1 teaspoon kosher salt

1 teaspoon ground cinnamon

1 teaspoon baking soda

½ teaspoon baking powder

Heat oven to 350 degrees. Grease a 9x5–inch loaf pan. Place lemon zest in a small bowl with 2 tablespoons sugar and mix with your fingers to release the lemon oil into the sugar.

Use your hands to squeeze the zucchini over the kitchen sink to wring out excess moisture. Place zucchini in a bowl with olive oil, butter, eggs, remaining ½ cup granulated sugar, brown sugar, vanilla, and lemon juice.

In a separate bowl, combine flour, salt, cinnamon, baking soda, and baking powder. Mix the dry ingredients with the wet ingredients until just combined.

Pour batter into the prepared loaf pan and smooth the top. Sprinkle with the lemon zest and sugar mixture. Bake for 55–60 minutes, until a toothpick inserted into the middle of the cake comes out clean.

NOTE: For muffins, bake for 25 minutes at 350 degrees. For mini loaves, bake for 28–30 minutes at 350 degrees.

Lemon Curd Tart

Serves 8

I love lemon bars and lemon desserts. The first time I made a tart, it was a lemon tart with a crust pressed into the pan. At the time, I was afraid to make the dough, and a pressed crust seemed like an easier way to go. That first tart was delicious, and I was very proud of it even though the filling leaked over the sides where the crust had slumped into the pan. I learned to do crust properly over time (I realized husband Kurt did not have to be the only person in our house who could make the pastry). I started with an apple pie and then took a pie-making class. I'm much better at tarts and pies now, and while Kurt still makes many of the galettes on True North Island, I make them at home with my own pastry recipe.

For crust

½ cup (1 stick) unsalted butter, cut into ½-inch cubes

1 large egg yolk

1 teaspoon granulated sugar

1¼ cups all-purpose flour

½ teaspoon kosher salt

3 tablespoons ice water, divided

1 tablespoon vodka

dried beans, for blind baking

For filling

zest of 3 lemons

1 cup fresh lemon juice

1½ cups granulated sugar

6 large eggs

pinch kosher salt

¾ cup (1½ sticks) butter, cut into pats

For serving

sugar-coated blueberries, fresh raspberries, candied lemon peels, fresh blueberries, or berry compote

For crust

Place the butter, egg yolk, sugar, flour, and salt in a food processor and pulse for 30–60 seconds or until the mixture has a coarse consistency. Add 2 tablespoons water and pulse 2 to 3 times. The dough should start to come together. Add the remaining water and vodka and pulse 6 more times. When the dough has reached the proper consistency, it will start to form a rough ball. Dump it onto a clean work surface dusted with flour. Form the dough into a disk, wrap in plastic wrap, and refrigerate for at least 30 minutes.

On a lightly floured work surface, roll out the dough to ⅛- to ¼-inch thickness. Lay the dough in a tart pan. Push the dough into the sides of the pan and run the rolling pin over the top to remove excess dough. Cover the dough with aluminum foil and gently poke the foil into the sides of the pan. (This step keeps the sides of the tart tall and straight as it bakes, which prevents the dough sides from slumping.) Refrigerate dough for 30 minutes.

Heat oven to 425 degrees. Fill the tart shell with dried beans (save and reuse the beans for this purpose) and place in the oven for 10 minutes. Remove the foil and beans and bake for 4 minutes more. Remove the tart shell from the oven and cool. The dough should be crisp and lightly golden.

For filling

Heat oven to 300 degrees. In a bowl, whisk together the lemon zest, lemon juice, sugar, eggs, and salt. Pour into a saucepan and set over medium heat. Cook, whisking constantly, until the mixture has thickened, about 12 minutes. Remove from heat and whisk in the butter, 1 pat at a time, until butter is fully incorporated and the mixture has a silky consistency.

Pour the curd into the prepared tart shell and bake until the filling has set, about 15 minutes. Let cool completely before cutting, about 45 minutes.

For serving

Decorate with sugar-coated blueberries, plain raspberries, or candied lemon peels or serve blueberries or a berry compote alongside.

Burntside Beach Pie

Serves 8

When I first read about Atlantic Beach Pie, what appealed to me most was the pie crust made with saltine crackers. I eat saltines with butter almost every day. With this pie an almost salted caramel–like flavor in the custard pairs well with the crust. No need to have a house in the Hamptons for this delicious pie.

For crust

1½ sleeves saltine crackers (about 60 crackers), crushed (see tip)

3 tablespoons granulated sugar

¾ cup (1½ sticks) unsalted butter, softened

For filling

1 (14-ounce) can sweetened condensed milk

2 large eggs plus 3 large egg yolks

½ cup fresh lemon and lime juice (approximately 1 lemon and 1 lime)

For serving

about 1 cup heavy cream, whipped

coarse sea salt

For crust

Heat oven to 350 degrees. Add cracker crumbs and sugar to a medium bowl. Knead in the butter until the crumbs hold together like dough. Press into an 8-inch pie pan using a small glass to press into the side and create a crisp edge and flat bottom. Chill in the freezer for 15 minutes. Bake for 18 minutes or until the crust has a little color. If the crust has slumped, use the glass to reshape while crust is hot. Set aside to cool.

For filling

In a medium bowl, beat together sweetened condensed milk, eggs, and egg yolks, then beat in the citrus juice until well combined. It is important to completely combine these ingredients. Pour into the baked pie crust and return to the oven for 16 minutes, until the filling has set. Let cool.

For serving

Chill pie completely. Serve with fresh whipped cream and a sprinkle of sea salt.

TIP: To prepare the crackers, use a food processor to grind them into crumbles or put them in a plastic bag and crush with a rolling pin.

Brittany's Banana Cream Pie

Serves 8

Each summer Brittany Johnson comes to visit her dad, Erik (husband Kurt's brother), at True North Island, and we often overlap. When she was a little girl, she loved to make banana cream pie from a boxed mix bought at Zup's grocery store. She simply added milk to make a sweet banana pudding, then poured the pudding into a graham cracker crust, and topped it with whipped cream and slices of fresh banana. While Brittany's version was delicious, I decided to give it an upgrade with the saltine cracker crust used in Burntside Beach Pie (page 156) and homemade custard.

For crust

1½ sleeves saltine crackers (about 60 crackers), crushed (see tip, page 156)

3 tablespoons granulated sugar

¾ cup (1½ sticks) unsalted butter, softened

For filling

1¾ cups whole milk

½ cup heavy cream

½ cup granulated sugar

¼ teaspoon kosher salt

4 large egg yolks

¼ cup cornstarch, sifted

1 teaspoon vanilla extract

2 tablespoons unsalted butter

2 ripe bananas, sliced

For serving

2 cups heavy cream

2 tablespoons confectioners' sugar

sea salt

For crust

Heat oven to 350 degrees. Add cracker crumbs and sugar to a medium bowl. Knead in the butter until the crumbs hold together like dough. Press into an 8-inch pie pan using a small glass to press into the side and create a crisp edge and flat bottom. Chill in the freezer for 15 minutes. Bake for 18 minutes or until the crust has a little color. If the crust has slumped, reshape with the glass while crust is hot. Let the crust cool for 30 minutes.

For filling

In a medium saucepan over medium heat, combine the milk, heavy cream, sugar, and salt. Whisk until all the sugar has dissolved, then bring to a gentle simmer. In a medium heat-proof bowl, whisk together the egg yolks and cornstarch until thick and smooth. Very slowly, add ½ cup of the simmering milk from the saucepan to the bowl to slightly warm the egg yolk mixture. Stir to incorporate, then add ¼ cup more. Stir again, then add another ¼ cup. Slowly pour mixture back into the saucepan, whisking continuously. (The goal is to avoid scrambling the eggs by heating them too quickly.) Continue cooking until mixture thickens, with big bubbles bursting at the surface, about 1 minute. Remove from the heat and whisk in the vanilla and butter.

To assemble

Line the bottom of the baked pie crust with the sliced bananas. Pour the filling over the bananas and refrigerate the pie for at least 4 hours.

For serving

Beat the cream and confectioners' sugar with an electric mixer until soft peaks form. Serve pie with fresh whipped cream piped on top or heaped onto the pie and spread with a spatula. Add a sprinkle of sea salt to finish.

Stephanie March's Napkin Custard for Homemade Ice Cream

Serves 6

We bought a Cuisinart ice cream maker for the cabin — none of that hand turning with lots of ice and rock salt. After a few failed attempts at getting the right consistency, I was having a burger with my radio show partner, Stephanie March, on a Saturday afternoon when she shared her custard base for the perfect ice cream maker ice cream. She wrote her recipe on a napkin. I have used this custard base ever since. Once you get the custard base set, you can add in fruit, nuts, cookies, or candy bits.

1 cup whole milk

1 cup half-and-half

6 large egg yolks

1 cup granulated sugar

Warm the milk and half-and-half in a medium saucepan on low heat. Beat the egg yolks with the sugar to a consistency of bright and creamy yellow ribbons. Slowly pour a thin stream of hot milk into the eggs while whisking continuously until combined. Return the combined milk and eggs to the pot and heat over medium-high heat, stirring occasionally, until thick enough to coat the back of a spoon. Remove from heat and let cool to room temperature, then refrigerate.

Add flavors (see variations below); pour into ice cream maker and start the machine. Within 25 minutes the mixture should be a creamy soft serve texture. Place the ice cream into a freezer-safe container to set for several hours, or freeze overnight for a harder ice cream.

VARIATIONS
Raspberry puree, fresh bananas and peanut butter, Dutch processed cocoa, fresh strawberries or blueberries, toffee pieces, and chocolate chips are all fun mix-in ideas.

Ellie's Molten Chocolate Cakes

Serves 8

Along with Teriyaki Steak (page 150), daughter Ellie has me make this gooey chocolate treat for her birthday. This recipe is adapted from Nigella Lawson's "Chocolate Hot Pots" that my friend Carrie Augst shared with me. Carrie heard me talking about my lack of success with this simple dessert and assured me Nigella's recipe truly is easy. It took me a couple years to get it right (Ellie doesn't pull her punches), but I finally developed a recipe that is almost foolproof. Of course, what makes the chocolate cakes molten is the gooey center, so the trick is to pull the cakes from the oven before the inside gets un-gooey. I make sure the top is cooked and slightly cracked, then check the center with a toothpick. It should come away coated (just the opposite of a typical cake). This is the dessert for those who love eating cake batter or raw cookie dough.

1 cup (2 sticks) unsalted butter, plus 8 teaspoons butter for ramekins

1 (10-ounce) package bittersweet baking chips (Ghirardelli 60 percent cacao)

4 large eggs

1½ cups superfine sugar

6 tablespoons all-purpose flour

½ teaspoon vanilla extract

kosher salt or sea salt flakes (Maldon)

8 medium-size ramekins that will hold about ⅔ cup batter

Place a baking sheet in the oven and heat to 400 degrees. Generously grease each ramekin with approximately 1 teaspoon of butter.

In a double boiler or in a metal or glass bowl suspended over a pan of simmering water (the bowl should not touch the water), melt the chocolate and 1 cup butter, stirring to combine. Set aside to cool for 5 minutes.

In another bowl, mix the eggs with the sugar, flour, and vanilla. Combine the two mixtures, beating with a whisk until thoroughly combined. Divide the batter among the prepared ramekins. Top with a sprinkle of salt.

Remove baking sheet from oven. Place ramekins on sheet, and bake for about 20 minutes, until the tops are cracked and the chocolate is still gooey underneath. Place each ramekin on a small plate with a teaspoon and serve. Be sure to warn people these desserts are molten hot.

Quick-Pickled Jalapeños

Makes 1 (16-ounce) jar

When we started our Hilltop Garden we planted red bell peppers, green bell peppers, banana peppers, and jalapeños. After a few years of trial and error we've shifted to planting only jalapeños. They're the one pepper that grows quickly enough in our Zone 3 climate. I love to pickle them. We use these for tacos, quesadillas, and burritos and in rice bowls with whatever I can scour from the refrigerator and kitchen shelves.

5 jalapeños, thinly sliced

1 clove garlic, peeled and smashed

⅔ cup distilled white vinegar

⅓ cup water

1 tablespoon granulated sugar

1 tablespoon kosher salt

Place the jalapeños and garlic in a large (16-ounce) Mason jar and place the jar on a potholder or heat-safe surface. In a small saucepan over low heat, simmer the vinegar, water, sugar, and salt, stirring occasionally, until the sugar is dissolved, about 5 minutes. Pour the hot brine over the jalapeños. Let cool to room temperature. Cover and chill for at least 30 minutes. These will last 2 weeks in the refrigerator and get spicier the longer they sit.

Simple Sauerkraut

Makes 1 quart

I was really excited to grow cabbages in Ely. There's a large Czech population in town, and sauerkraut is plentiful at stores in the area. Zup's makes its own brand of sauerkraut that's delicious, but I wanted to try to make it myself. I learned a lot from a book by Amanda Feifer called *Ferment Your Vegetables*. I found her on Instagram (@phicklefoods), and she ferments everything, so I thought I'd give it a shot with three of the beautiful cabbages I grew. At first I used Mason jars with weights to hold everything down. I tried special lids for off-gassing that seemed to work pretty well, but I was always nervous about opening them and letting in too many germs. What I've settled on is Mason jars with weights and plastic tops that let the carbon dioxide out but keep the pesky bacteria from getting in. If you get a little white mold on top of your kraut, just pick it off. But if the mold turns pink or red, you shouldn't eat that batch.

1 large head of cabbage to yield 8 cups shredded

4 teaspoons kosher salt

Core cabbage and remove any outer damaged leaves. Reserve 1 cabbage leaf. Shred cabbage into ¼-inch strips. Place shredded cabbage in a large bowl, add salt, and toss thoroughly for 1 minute. Let the cabbage sit for 20 minutes.

After 20 minutes, massage the cabbage for 3 minutes. When there is a puddle of water in the bottom of the bowl and the cabbage pieces stay in a loose clump when squeezed, it's time to pack the jar. Press the cabbage into the bottom of a 1-quart wide-mouth Mason jar, and pack it along the sides and bottom, until it comes to about 1 inch below the jar rim. Press down firmly to release juices and eliminate air pockets.

Place the reserved cabbage leaf on top of the kraut and press the sides of the leaf around the edges of the shredded cabbage, creating a surface barrier. Place weights on top or otherwise make sure the shredded cabbage is submerged under the surface barrier cabbage leaf. Loosely place the jar lid on, but don't tighten completely. Allow to ferment at room temperature for 4–6 weeks.

Keep the cabbage submerged in the brine it releases to keep oxygen out and prevent mold growth. Check weekly to make sure the brine level is still above the top of the cabbage. If it isn't, press down on the top cabbage leaf to bring the brine back above. Mold is a normal part of the process. White, blue, and green mold can be scraped off with a spoon. If the mold is black or pink, dump the batch and start over.

Once the taste is to your preference, remove the leaf, secure the jar lid, and place the jar in the fridge.

Quick Cabin Refrigerator Pickles

Makes 1 quart

These pickles are great to make when the cucumbers first start coming into the garden. They're perfect for burgers, in tartar sauce for fried walleye, or just for snacking. Refrigerator pickles will keep for three weeks, *if* they last that long.

1 cup water

1 cup distilled white vinegar

2 tablespoons granulated sugar

2 teaspoons kosher salt

¼ cup fresh dill, divided

2 medium cloves garlic, peeled and smashed

2 medium garden cucumbers, cut into ½-inch rounds

½ teaspoon crushed red pepper

1 teaspoon freshly ground black pepper

In a small saucepan combine the water, vinegar, sugar, and salt. Heat until the sugar and salt dissolve. Pour mixture into a liquid measuring cup and let cool to room temperature.

Place half the dill and 1 garlic clove in the bottom of a 1-quart wide-mouth Mason jar. Stack the cucumbers in the jar. Top the cucumbers with the remaining dill, garlic, crushed red pepper, and freshly ground black pepper. Pour the liquid over the cucumbers so they're fully submerged. Cover and refrigerate for at least 1 day before serving. These pickles will keep for up to 3 weeks refrigerated, and their flavor will continue to develop.

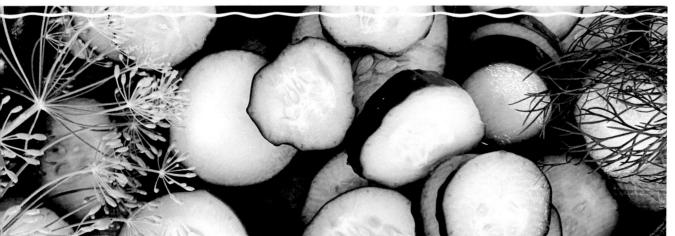

HILLTOP

The cabin on True North Island is built for summer, with single-pane windows, zero insulation, and one fireplace for warmth. Our water is pumped from the lake. Temperatures in Ely often dip below freezing in September, and the chill can lead to busted pipes, so when Labor Day arrives, it's time to close up for the season.

After a summer of cooking, the cabinets are emptied of any items containing liquids that will freeze and burst over the winter months. Cans of tomato sauce, bottles of hot sauce, mini cans of V8 bloody Mary mix all make it home, while half-eaten bags of crackers and semi-hard marshmallows for s'mores get tossed. We empty the refrigerator. Dijon mustard, at least two bottles of ketchup, and various partially full jars of jams are packed up, along with anything left in the freezer — stock frozen in Mason jars and half-eaten packages of Zup's Polish delights. It amazes me how gross a refrigerator can get after only five months of use. My husband, Kurt, pulls the water hose from the lake and drains all the pipes beneath the cabin. Our dog, Nikki, seems to know what's going on, looks a little morose, and stands near the boat hoping we won't depart without her. She's very quiet, though, and once, by accident, in the hustle and bustle of getting the boat docked, the trash thrown out, and the car packed, we did leave her behind. Halfway home, we stopped for lunch and realized she wasn't with us. We turned around and drove back to the marina, where Nikki was sitting in the boat, patiently waiting for us.

It's always sad to close the cabin, but autumn is also a beautiful time in Ely. The lake is quiet with most of the summer people gone, the air is cool and crisp, and the trees start to turn. The birch leaves look like flecks of gold in the sunlight, and the maples high on surrounding bluffs begin to burn red and orange. But our time in Ely doesn't end immediately. We move up to our cabin on the shore, Hilltop, and the final garden harvest that awaits.

In 2015 Kurt and I purchased Hilltop, a shore-view property across from the island with lake access to Burntside. In fact, we can see dock to dock from the True North Island property to Hilltop. We found the parcel on Craigslist and were surprised because it was the cheapest property ever listed on the lake. The cabin, only twenty years old, was small, with just one bedroom, but the eat-in kitchen was large, and the living room could easily be turned into a second bedroom. It had indoor plumbing with a well that served up cold spring water and a septic system — both luxuries for islanders used to pumping water from the lake and using a stinky outhouse (no matter how nice we kept it). The cabin resided on seven acres of wooded land that backed up to Superior National Forest. What was the catch? Why was the property so cheap? The lake and dock were at the end of a narrow, twelve-foot-wide deeded access through a neighbor's property. The cabin and seven acres were at the top of the hill on the other side of the main road. The climb from the lakeshore dock to the cabin was over a thousand feet straight up. Hence the name: Hilltop.

Hilltop has stretched our time up north into the fall, winter, and spring seasons. We watch the maples on our property turn crimson and gold, and in winter we cross-country ski and snowmobile along the forest trails (with a stop for a bloody Mary at Benchwarmers Sports Grille in Tower, Minnesota). In the spring, we can see the lake ice go out from our Hilltop perch. We watch deer, pine marten, wolves on the ice, birds — and even bears.

Once I made the mistake of putting out a bird feeder filled with thistle, which attracted few birds but one hefty bear. The shepherd's hook on which the feeder hung was set up right outside the living room window, and I watched as the bear walked up to the feeder, sniffed around, then casually bent the steel pole over like a pipe cleaner. He tore open the plastic feeder with his paws and jaws and began eating the thistle. Kurt was in the garage, and I tried to text him a warning, but he didn't have his phone. I watched as Kurt walked up the driveway and saw the bear. Kurt stopped, watched, then yelled, "Hey, hey!" The bear barely looked in his direction. Kurt came in and took out two saucepans from the kitchen. He went back outside and began banging the pans and shouting. The bear looked his way but kept on eating the bird-

seed, undeterred. Finally, we just waited until the bear was finished and sauntered off. I now feed birds only during the winter when the chickadees and blue jays are out and the bears are hibernating deep beneath the cover of snow.

We have a vegetable garden at Hilltop surrounded by a six-foot fence to keep the bears and deer out. I'd never had a garden or knew anything about cultivating cucumbers, cabbages, peas, onions, lettuces, zucchini, beans, beets, tomatoes, asparagus, and everything that grows in

our cold weather zone. I'm now in my third year, and I've started to get the hang of it. As I write these lines in late June, we've already eaten the spring asparagus, the first crop of radishes, and some of the early greens like spinach and arugula. I've found that I like gardening, and it gives me immense joy to plan, plant, weed, watch things grow, harvest, cook, and eat fresh from the Hilltop Garden.

One piece of advice for Ely gardeners is to grow Early Girl tomatoes. Even the earliest fruits don't come in until late August or early September, and then I work furiously to pick what I can before the first frost hits. A favorite recipe is a simple Tomato Pie (page 196), with layers of fresh tomatoes cooked in a flaky pastry crust and topped with Parmesan cheese. Of course, I love fresh tomatoes, sometimes drizzled

with olive oil and sprinkled with salt. But there are just too many tomatoes for us to eat or even give away. I like to dry much of the rest in the oven, add a little olive oil, and freeze or blend into a simple sauce (pages 182 and 184) that we use for spaghetti or roasted tomato soup. The drying process reduces the tomatoes' volume and condenses their flavor. We use the dried and frozen tomatoes throughout the winter for sauces, soups, pasta, and risotto, adding seasonings based on the dish we're cooking. Eating tomatoes in winter is a comfortable reminder of the next season to come on True North Island and Hilltop.

Apple Cider Cocktail

Serves 1

Apple cider makes its return after Labor Day each fall, and I am always ready. I particularly love Pepin Heights Honeycrisp Apple Cider.

3 (3-inch) apple wedges

1 lime wedge

1½ ounces vodka

⅓ cup apple cider

cinnamon stick, for garnish

soda water

Add 2 apple wedges and lime wedge to a cocktail shaker and muddle to extract their juices. Shake with vodka and apple cider. Strain into an ice-filled glass, and garnish with a cinnamon stick or remaining apple wedge. Top with soda water.

Maple Old Fashioned

Serves 1

My husband, Kurt, stumbled upon this recipe after never seeming to have simple syrup on the island and getting tired of making it himself (though it's pretty simple: equal parts water and granulated sugar, boiled). He discovered maple syrup makes a tasty substitute for simple syrup. Kurt initially used Log Cabin syrup, but I'm a purist at heart and will never make this recipe without real maple syrup. Kurt doesn't waste the good bourbon that should be sipped neat like Maker's Mark or Woodford Reserve. He's fine with the Evan Williams you can find on the bottom shelf of your neighborhood liquor store.

2 ounces bourbon

½ ounce maple syrup

2 dashes Angostura bitters

2 dashes orange bitters

orange peel and cherry, for garnish

Stir bourbon, syrup, and bitters in a rocks glass. Add ice. Garnish with orange peel and cherry.

Sage Gimlet

Serves 1

Aquavit is what makes this cocktail special. This Nordic spirit is enjoyed throughout Scandinavia, particularly at holidays, chilled or at room temperature, straight up in a small liqueur glass. Here I prefer it mixed, though I'm not opposed to doing a shot when a festive occasion arises. Gamle Ode in Wisconsin makes a lovely dill aquavit that gives this cocktail the herbaceous yin to the lime's yang. The sage leaf floating on top makes the presentation particularly elegant, but a sprig of dill would be at home here too.

2 ounces aquavit

1 ounce fresh lime juice

1 ounce simple syrup

3 sage leaves

Add the aquavit, lime juice, simple syrup, and 2 sage leaves to a shaker, then add ice. Shake well, then strain into a coupe glass. Garnish with remaining sage leaf.

Split Pea and Ham Soup

Serves 6

Pea soup is one of those meals young couples learn to cook during the broke years early in their relationship. It's simple, delicious, and easy to make in a slow cooker, Instant Pot, or Dutch oven. The package of peas costs pennies, and the smoked ham hock is cheaper than ground beef. A thick pea soup served with French bread and butter is a hearty meal. I once served this humble soup for a winter dinner party I had with chef Jack Riebel (of The Lexington fame; rest in peace, friend) and his wife, Kat. I recall him saying how people were always trying to impress him with a fancy meal when he sometimes just loved a simple, tasty bowl of soup.

Pea soup was particularly delicious after Christmas Day when my mother served honey-glazed ham. Kurt and I would be given leftovers along with the ham bone, which none of my sisters even considered. So, imagine a young couple on a snowy evening curled up in front of a good movie (I love *Gone with the Wind*; my husband, *Lawrence of Arabia*), eating meaty pea soup with crusty bread, then maybe a little buttered Cabin Caramel Corn (page 207). What could be better than that?

1 tablespoon extra-virgin olive oil

1½ cups chopped yellow onion

3 ribs celery with leaves, chopped

1½ cups chopped carrots

2 cloves garlic, minced

8 cups (2 quarts) chicken broth

1 (16-ounce) bag split peas

1 bay leaf

2 teaspoons chopped fresh thyme leaves

2 teaspoons kosher salt

1 teaspoon black pepper

meaty ham bone or shank

1 tablespoon chopped Italian flat-leaf parsley

Heat olive oil in a large stockpot or Dutch oven over medium-high heat. Add onions, celery, and carrots and cook, stirring, for 4 minutes. Add garlic and cook and stir 1 minute longer. Pour in chicken broth. Add split peas, bay leaf, and thyme. Stir in salt and pepper. Nestle ham bone into soup mixture. Bring mixture to a boil, then reduce to low. Cover and let simmer, stirring occasionally, until peas and ham are tender, about 1½ hours. Remove the ham bone from the soup, let it cool, then shred or dice the ham. Stir diced ham into the soup and add parsley. Taste and adjust seasonings.

White Bean, Sage, and Ham Hock Soup

Serves 8

This is another hearty soup that should be in your cabin repertoire. When the soup is simmering on the stove and the smell is wafting throughout the cabin, you can hardly wait for the dinner bell.

1 tablespoon extra-virgin olive oil

1 medium white onion, finely chopped

2 carrots, finely chopped

1 rib celery, finely chopped

2 cloves garlic, chopped

2 teaspoons dried sage

1 teaspoon fresh thyme leaves

1 teaspoon chopped fresh rosemary leaves

3 cups chopped ham (or a bacon-smoked ham hock)

8 cups (2 quarts) chicken broth

1 (16-ounce) package dried great northern beans, soaked overnight for 6–8 hours in 6 cups of cold water

2 teaspoons kosher salt

1 teaspoon black pepper

¼ cup chopped Italian flat-leaf parsley

Heat a Dutch oven over medium heat and add olive oil, onions, carrots, and celery. Cook and stir for 5 minutes. Add garlic, sage, thyme, and rosemary and cook for 3 minutes more. Add the ham or ham bone and broth. Cover and bring to a boil, then reduce heat to medium-low and simmer for 30 minutes.

Drain the beans and add them to the pot. Simmer, uncovered, for 2 hours or until beans are soft and tender. If using a ham bone, remove, let cool, pick ham from bone, and add meat back into the soup. Season with salt and pepper and add fresh parsley.

TIP: If the soup is thin, thicken by using a potato masher to crush some of the beans.

Zucchini Soup with Curry and Apple

Serves 6

This soup is a lovely way to use up lots of zucchini, including squash that may be blemished or past its prime. This recipe can easily be made in an Instant Pot (see note). Top with a dollop of sour cream to add some richness.

2 tablespoons extra-virgin olive oil

2 tablespoons butter

1 large yellow onion, chopped

1 cup grated Honeycrisp apple

1 tablespoon curry powder

2 teaspoons kosher salt

4 cups zucchini cut into 1-inch chunks (about 3 medium or 2 large zucchini)

4 cups (1 quart) chicken or vegetable stock

cracked black pepper

Heat olive oil and butter in a stockpot over medium heat. Add onions, apple, curry powder, and salt. Stir and cook for about 4 minutes, until onions become translucent. Add zucchini and cook for 5 more minutes. Add stock and stir to combine. Cook on low for 15 minutes. Use an immersion blender to blend soup in the pot until smooth. Finish with freshly cracked black pepper.

NOTE: To make in an Instant Pot, cook onions, apple, and zucchini in olive oil and butter for 5 minutes on the sauté setting. Add the curry powder, salt, and stock to the pot. Pressure cook for 2 minutes on high. Pressurizing will take about 12 minutes, and then the 2-minute timer will begin. Once the timer is done, manually let off the remaining steam (quick release). Use an immersion blender to blend soup in the Instant Pot until smooth. Finish with freshly cracked black pepper.

Creamy Roasted Tomato Basil Soup

Serves 6

At the beginning of the pandemic, my five-day-a-week habit of eating out abruptly stopped, and I was home-bound with the rest of the nation. In December 2020, after so many of us had not been working out in a gym for ten months, cookies and other holiday treats were less welcome than in years past. My cookie exchange was canceled, and I missed seeing my friends, so I decided to do a soup drop to deliver some holiday cheer. With quarts of roasted, blended tomatoes on hand from the Hilltop Garden, I set to work making my version of roasted tomato basil soup (adapted from the queen, Ina Garten, aka the Barefoot Contessa). The smiles on my friends' faces when I showed up with quarts of soup has converted me into someone who gives soup instead of cookies at the holidays. I give soup as a housewarming present or for new babies or folks who get sick, and I still do yearly holiday soup drops.

12 Roma tomatoes, cut in half lengthwise

4 tablespoons extra-virgin olive oil, divided

1 tablespoon kosher salt

freshly ground coarse black pepper

2 tablespoons unsalted butter

2 cups chopped yellow onion

4 cloves garlic, minced

1 teaspoon crushed red pepper

1 (28-ounce) can plum tomatoes with their juice (see tip)

2 cups packed fresh basil leaves

1 teaspoon fresh thyme leaves

4 cups (1 quart) chicken stock

1 cup heavy cream, optional

Heat oven to 400 degrees. Spread the halved tomatoes on a rimmed baking sheet in a single layer and drizzle with 2 tablespoons olive oil. Sprinkle with kosher salt and 10 grinds of coarse black pepper. Roast for 45 minutes.

In an 8-quart stockpot over medium heat, melt butter and add remaining 2 tablespoons olive oil. Cook the onions and garlic with crushed red pepper, stirring often, for 10 minutes, until the onions start to brown. Add the canned tomatoes and juices, basil, thyme, and chicken stock. Add the oven-roasted tomatoes, including the liquid on the baking sheet. Bring to a boil and simmer, uncovered, for 40 minutes. Blend in a Vitamix or blender (be careful to vent the top hole of the blender by, for example, covering with a dish towel). Finish by stirring in cream, if using.

TIP: Substitute 2 cups or a pint Mason jar of Oven-Dried Roasted Garden Tomatoes (page 182); increase the stock to 5 cups.

Maple Praline Walnut, Cranberry, and Apple Salad with Maple-Dijon Vinaigrette

Serves 6

This is my go-to fall salad. It's great to serve when you have company or as a pairing with your favorite fall soup.

For walnuts

4 cups raw walnut pieces

½ cup maple syrup

1 teaspoon kosher salt

½ teaspoon cayenne

For vinaigrette

⅓ cup extra-virgin olive oil

2 tablespoons maple syrup

2 tablespoons fresh lemon juice

1 tablespoon Dijon mustard

½ teaspoon kosher salt

8 grinds freshly cracked black pepper

For salad

6 cups mixed baby greens

2 apples, seeded, cut into bite-size wedges

½ cup dried cranberries

For walnuts

Prepare a baking sheet by lining with a baking mat or parchment paper. Add nuts to a medium or large dry cast iron skillet set over medium-high heat. Toast nuts until they become brown in spots and smell roasty, about 3–5 minutes.

When the nuts are done roasting, add maple syrup to the pan and turn the burner to low, stirring nuts to coat evenly with maple syrup. The maple syrup will begin to bubble within a couple of minutes; this is the beginning of the caramelization process. Quickly salt the nuts and sprinkle on the cayenne. Keep stirring while they are caramelizing: the syrup will begin to harden and turn to caramel, sticking to the nuts in the hot pan. When there is no more bubbling, remove from heat immediately. Do not burn! Pour nuts onto prepared pan in an even layer and let them cool and harden.

For vinaigrette

Shake ingredients in a Mason jar until thoroughly combined.

For salad

Arrange greens on a pretty platter or divide among 6 salad plates. Decorate with apples, cranberries, and praline walnuts. Just before serving, drizzle with vinaigrette.

Chicken, Wild Rice, and Apple-Pecan Salad

Serves 4

I like serving this salad in the fall when the leaves start changing. The combination of wild rice and apples always feels right for the season, and this is a handy salad for a light dinner or as a weekday lunch when you're working from home. You can also substitute leftover roasted chicken.

For vinaigrette

2 large cloves garlic, minced or grated

⅓ cup rice vinegar

¼ cup toasted sesame oil

¼ cup extra-virgin olive oil

2 tablespoons soy sauce

1 tablespoon Dijon mustard

1 teaspoon orange zest

1 tablespoon fresh orange juice

1 tablespoon grated fresh ginger

1 teaspoon kosher salt

1 teaspoon black pepper

For salad

2 cups wild rice

2 boneless chicken breasts

1 teaspoon salt

4½ cups chicken stock

½ cup raw pecans

1 cup cubed Honeycrisp apple

2 ribs celery with leaves, chopped

1 cup chopped green onions, light green and white parts

½ cup chopped red onion

¼ cup chopped Italian flat-leaf parsley

For vinaigrette

Place all ingredients in a Mason jar and shake until thoroughly combined.

For salad

Place the wild rice in a saucepan. Arrange the chicken in a single layer on top of the rice. Add salt and stock to the pot and bring to a boil. (White scummy foam will collect on the surface of the stock; it's fine to leave it.) Reduce heat to a simmer, cover, and let the chicken and rice cook for 15 minutes. Remove the chicken from the pot and set aside to cool. Continue cooking rice for another 30 minutes.

Meanwhile, toast the pecans in a dry cast iron skillet over medium heat until fragrant and brown. (The nuts will burn easily, so pay close attention.) Set aside.

Cut chicken into ½-inch cubes. Drain rice and set aside to cool.

In a large mixing bowl, toss apple cubes with vinaigrette. Add cubed chicken, rice, celery, green onions, red onion, parsley, and toasted pecans. Toss again until all the ingredients are well coated.

Oven-Dried Roasted Garden Tomatoes

Makes approximately 8-10 cups

When I have lots of tomatoes from the Hilltop Garden and typically one week to deal with the harvest, I find ways to cook, can, and otherwise preserve them to get through the fall and winter. I demonstrated this recipe on *The Jason Show* here in the Twin Cities and in Seattle, and since then folks have resorted to calling me the Tomato Lady. I use these tomatoes in soups, in stews, blended as the base for spaghetti and meatballs, or in my Creamy Roasted Tomato Basil Soup (page 178). They're also great with risotto, or as a dip with feta or goat cheese roasted in a cast iron skillet.

5 pounds (approximately 40) Roma tomatoes (see tip), halved

2 tablespoons sea salt

2 tablespoons extra-virgin olive oil

Heat oven to 225 degrees. Arrange tomatoes cut side up on a rimmed baking sheet. Sprinkle with sea salt and drizzle the pan with olive oil. Bake for 3½ hours, then check for juiciness. The texture may be "roasted and condensed": good for tomato sauce. Or bake 2 more hours for "sun-dried" consistency.

TIP: Early Girls work too. They make more sauce because they are larger than Romas.

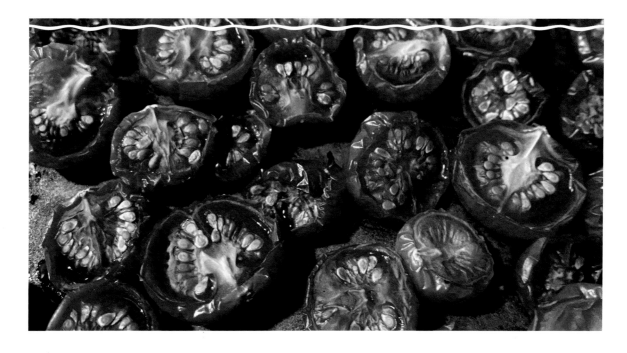

Oven-Dried Tomato Risotto

Serves 4

This recipe calls for two cups of Oven-Dried Roasted Garden Tomatoes (page 182).

4 cups (1 quart) chicken or vegetable stock

¼ cup extra-virgin olive oil

2 tablespoons butter

1 cup finely chopped onion

2 cloves garlic, minced

1 cup arborio rice

2 cups Oven-Dried Roasted Garden Tomatoes (page 182)

2 tablespoons chopped fresh herbs (parsley, basil, chives, thyme, oregano)

salt and black pepper

¼ cup grated Parmesan cheese, plus more for serving

In a medium saucepan, bring stock to a simmer and keep warm. In a large saucepan over medium heat, add olive oil, butter, and onions. Cook until onions are translucent, about 7 minutes. Add garlic and rice and cook, stirring, for 2 minutes more.

Add hot broth to rice mixture, ½ cup at a time, stirring until incorporated and absorbed by the rice. After adding 2 cups of broth, stir in the roasted tomatoes. Continue adding broth, ½ cup at a time, stirring until incorporated, using just enough broth to reach desired consistency. The process of adding broth and stirring until absorbed takes about 15 minutes.

When the rice is done, remove from the heat and add the fresh herbs, salt and pepper, and Parmesan cheese and stir to combine. Season to taste and serve with extra grated cheese at the table.

Oven-Dried Winter Tomato Sauce for Canning or Freezing

Makes roughly 2 quarts

This sauce is purposefully plain. When using it to make soup, stews, or sauce for pasta, feel free to add more salt and pepper and whatever flavorings or herbs you're feeling for that meal. If serving the sauce over pasta, I usually add one-third cup of chopped fresh basil and a few tablespoons of melted butter, like Marcella Hazan, the grandmother of all Italian cooking, did in her tomato butter sauce.

½ cup extra-virgin olive oil

1 teaspoon crushed red pepper

1 medium onion, chopped (about 1 cup)

1 cup chopped zucchini

½ cup chopped carrot

½ cup chopped celery, including leaves

8 cups (2 quarts) Oven-Dried Roasted Garden Tomatoes (page 182)

1 cup red wine

1 (11.5-ounce) can vegetable juice (V8)

2 teaspoons kosher salt

2 teaspoons black pepper

Heat the oil in a large Dutch oven over medium-high heat. Add the crushed red pepper and onions and cook, stirring, for 5 minutes. Add the zucchini, carrots, and celery and cook for about 5 minutes more. Add roasted tomatoes to the pot with red wine and vegetable juice and bring to a boil. Lower the heat to medium low.

Cook for about 30 minutes, until the sauce has reduced and thickened. (If it's reducing too fast, turn down the heat and cook it slower, or add a bit more red wine to loosen it up.) Remove from heat and stir in the salt and pepper. Allow to cool. Pour sauce into Mason jars, leaving 1–2 inches of space at the top. Freeze the sauce and use within 6 months, or can the sauce and use within 12 months.

For canning sauce

While the sauce is simmering, place jars and lids in a large pot that will hold jars upright, cover with water, and bring to a boil. Boil jars and lids for 10 minutes. Remove from the water and let air dry. Continue to boil water.

Fill the sanitized jars with the finished sauce, leaving 1 inch of space at the top. Fit jars with lids. Carefully lower the jars into the boiling water using a jar holder or tongs. Water should cover the jars by at least 1 inch. Boil for 40 minutes. Carefully lift jars out of the water bath and leave on the counter to cool for 12 hours or overnight. You might hear the "ping" of the jar lids sealing. The next day, check to be sure the jars have sealed by pushing on the center of the lid. The lid should not pop up or have any give.

If the lid flexes, it did not seal. Refrigerate the jar and use sauce within a few days, or scoop out a few tablespoons of sauce to leave more head room in the jar for expansion and freeze.

Lamb Ragout

Serves 4

This recipe is adapted from the 1962 edition of *The New York Times Cookbook*, edited by the renowned Craig Claiborne. From what I've been able to discern, this recipe has only ever appeared in that version of the cookbook and is not available online in the *New York Times* recipe archive. This recipe is a family favorite, and my mother-in-law, Dolores, makes it at the cabin every year. Over time I, too, started making it at the first sign of fall. If you like beef stew, you'll likely love lamb ragout.

¼ cup all-purpose flour

1 teaspoon kosher salt

1 teaspoon freshly cracked black pepper

2 pounds lamb stew meat, cut into 1½-inch cubes

¼ cup extra-virgin olive oil

1½ cups beef consommé (Campbell's)

⅓ cup Spanish sherry (or ¼ cup fresh lemon juice)

1 clove garlic, crushed

1 teaspoon lemon zest

2 tablespoons fresh lemon juice

2 tablespoons chopped parsley

12 ounces egg noodles, cooked according to package instructions

¼ cup grated Parmesan cheese

Heat oven to 350 degrees. In a zip-top bag combine the flour, salt, pepper, and lamb pieces. Seal the bag and shake to coat each piece.

Heat the olive oil in a Dutch oven and cook the prepared lamb cubes, stirring often, until browned on all sides. Add the beef consommé, sherry (or ¼ cup lemon juice), and garlic. Bake, covered, until the lamb is tender, about 1½ hours. Stir in lemon zest, 2 tablespoons lemon juice, and parsley to finish the stew.

Serve lamb ragout over egg noodles with grated Parmesan cheese to taste.

Grilled Lamb Burgers with Tzatziki Feta Sauce

Serves 4

Husband Kurt's brother, Erik, who lives in Canada, swears by lamb burgers over beef burgers, so Kurt's mom makes this delicious recipe for him each summer.

For sauce

- 1 small cucumber, peeled, sliced in half lengthwise, seeded
- 1 cup plain Greek yogurt
- 1 tablespoon fresh lemon juice
- 1 teaspoon mayonnaise
- 1 small clove garlic, minced or grated
- 1 tablespoon finely chopped fresh dill
- ¼ cup crumbled feta cheese
- 1 teaspoon kosher salt

For burgers

- 1 pound ground lamb
- ⅓ cup red onion grated on a box grater
- 2 cloves garlic, minced or grated
- 1 cup chopped fresh parsley
- ¼ cup chopped mint leaves
- 2 teaspoons dried oregano
- 1 teaspoon cumin
- ½ teaspoon paprika
- 1 teaspoon kosher salt
- 2 teaspoons extra-virgin olive oil
- 4 pita halves, for serving
- sliced tomatoes, cucumbers, and onions, for serving

For sauce

Finely chop cucumber so it's almost like a mash. Mix with yogurt, lemon juice, mayonnaise, garlic, dill, crumbled feta, and salt.

For burgers

Place the lamb in a mixing bowl. Add grated onion, garlic, parsley, mint, oregano, cumin, paprika, salt, and olive oil. Mix until everything is well combined. Divide the meat mixture into 4 equal portions and shape into patties.

Grill burgers over medium heat, covered, for 4–5 minutes on each side, until meat is cooked through and registers 160 degrees. Allow burgers to rest for 5–10 minutes before serving.

Serve in half a pita with a hearty dollop of sauce, sliced tomatoes, cucumbers, and onions.

Fresh Herb Salts

Makes 1 pint

We always have a pot of herbs growing on the island and more herbs planted in the garden at Hilltop. Fresh herb salts are a way to extend the flavors of the growing season. We use them on chicken and other meats and as a rub on our Thanksgiving turkey. I usually make herb salts with oregano, sage, thyme, rosemary, or parsley. Mint, cilantro, and basil also work, but I find that by late in the season the plants have bolted and the leaves are bitter.

3 cups herb of choice, coarse stems and discolored leaves removed

½ cup kosher salt

Blend herbs and salt in a food processor until combined. Store in a pint-size Mason jar in the refrigerator for up to 6 months.

Pork Shoulder with Sauerkraut and Kopytka (Potato Dumplings) with Horseradish Cream

Serves 6–8

My mother-in-law, Dolores, and I both love dumplings. Dolores's mom, Grandma Debower, made fantastic plum dumplings with the Italian black plums you can only get for a few weeks in August. Making them is typically a big production: cover the plums with dough, boil them, pan fry the dumplings in sugar and butter, and finally serve with pork. I love this recipe because it's much easier. My mother had a Polish nanny named Anna who made her potato dumplings, cooked simply in a Dutch oven with pork and sauerkraut. This recipe is one of the reasons I learned to make sauerkraut with the cabbage grown at the Hilltop Garden.

For sauerkraut

1 tablespoon extra-virgin olive oil

1 yellow onion, chopped

1 teaspoon fresh thyme leaves

1 teaspoon kosher salt

½ teaspoon black pepper

⅓ cup apple cider

4 cups sauerkraut and its juices, homemade or store-bought

1 cup chicken broth

For roast

2 teaspoons kosher salt

1 teaspoon black pepper

1 teaspoon smoked paprika

1 teaspoon caraway seeds

1 teaspoon thyme leaves, fresh or dried

1 (5- to 7-pound) pork shoulder

For horseradish cream

½ cup sour cream or plain full-fat Greek yogurt

½ cup prepared horseradish

¼ cup heavy cream

1 tablespoon fresh lemon juice

kosher salt to taste

For kopytka (potato dumplings)

4 medium Yukon Gold potatoes, peeled and quartered

1 large egg

about 1 cup all-purpose flour, plus more for rolling

1 teaspoon cornstarch

1 teaspoon kosher salt

For sauerkraut

Heat oven to 275 degrees. In a Dutch oven over medium-high heat, add olive oil and onions and cook, stirring, for 5 minutes. Add the thyme, salt, and pepper and stir to combine. Add the apple cider and stir, scraping up any browned bits from the pan. Remove from the heat.

Add the sauerkraut and its juices, then add chicken broth so braising liquid covers sauerkraut.

For roast

Combine seasonings and rub roast on all sides. Nestle the roast inside the Dutch oven on top of the sauerkraut, fat-side up. Score the fat cap with hash marks. Cover roast and cook for 6 hours or until the internal temperature has reached 145 degrees.

Meanwhile, prepare horseradish cream (see instructions at right).

When the roast is done, hoist it out of the Dutch oven and place it on a platter. Remove the fat cap (or leave it if it is crispy) and tent the roast to keep warm.

Increase oven temperature to 350 degrees. Start preparing dumplings (see instructions at right).

Assess the braising liquid: If there are large pools of fat on top, skim off with a ladle. If mixture seems dry, add another 1–2 cups chicken broth so braising liquid covers sauerkraut.

Prepare to add the dumplings to the pot. While they are cooking, slice roast.

For horseradish cream

Blend all ingredients until combined. Refrigerate for at least 30 minutes to let flavors meld.

For kopytka (potato dumplings)

Place potatoes in cold salted water. Bring to boiling and boil 15–20 minutes, until tender. Drain the potatoes and allow them to cool.

Process the potatoes in a food processor until smooth, about 30 seconds. Add egg, ¾ cup flour, cornstarch, and salt. Process until the ingredients are combined, about 30 seconds more. Add more flour if necessary, until the mixture becomes a soft dough.

Transfer the dough to a floured work surface, and knead until smooth and pliable. Cut a small chunk of the dough, about ½ cup, and use your hands to roll it out into a "snake" about 1 inch thick. Cut on the diagonal into approximately ½-inch dumplings. Repeat with remaining dough.

Lay dumplings atop sauerkraut, making sure there is enough liquid left in the pot for them to steam. Cover the Dutch oven and place in the oven to bake for 15 minutes.

Serve steamed dumplings alongside the sliced pork shoulder with sauerkraut and horseradish cream on the side.

Roasted Chicken with Olives, Rosemary, and Tomatoes

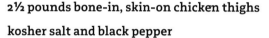

Serves 4

The flavor of chicken with olives, rosemary, and tomatoes, stewed and served over polenta or mashed potatoes, is so comforting. This dish makes the house smell amazing and will prepare you for seasonal treats like crusty bread and cups of apple cider. This is a great dish to assemble and then let the oven do the work while you take a nap.

2½ pounds bone-in, skin-on chicken thighs

kosher salt and black pepper

1 tablespoon extra-virgin olive oil

1 medium white onion, finely chopped

3 cloves garlic, minced

¼ cup capers

⅓ cup Worcestershire sauce

1 (28-ounce) can crushed tomatoes

1 cup pitted black olives

1 tablespoon brown sugar

1 teaspoon crushed red pepper

2 sprigs fresh rosemary

polenta, couscous, or mashed potatoes, for serving

Heat oven to 425 degrees. Season chicken thighs with kosher salt and black pepper. In a medium oven-safe skillet, heat the olive oil over high heat and brown the chicken thighs, starting with the skin side and then flipping. Remove from the pan and set aside.

Remove excess fat from the pan, leaving 1 teaspoon behind. Reduce the heat to medium, add onions and garlic, and cook, stirring, until browned. Stir in capers, Worcestershire sauce, crushed tomatoes, olives, brown sugar, and crushed red pepper, then add chicken. Tuck a few sprigs of rosemary among the chicken thighs. Bake, uncovered, for 25 minutes.

Serve with polenta, couscous, or mashed potatoes.

Roasted Cabbage Steaks

Makes 4 cabbage steaks

Cabbage, like parsnips, brussels sprouts, rutabaga, and celery root, is one of those vegetables that you think you don't like until someone roasts it to perfection. Try these easy-to-make cabbage planks to jump-start your love of cabbage. If you're serving kids, sprinkle a bit of grated Parmesan cheese on top about 10 minutes before the cabbage is done roasting (you may like it this way too).

1 small head cabbage, cored, cut into 1-inch-thick steaks

3 tablespoons extra-virgin olive oil

2 teaspoons kosher salt

1 teaspoon smoked paprika

1 teaspoon freshly cracked black pepper

1 teaspoon thyme leaves (fresh or dried)

fresh grated Parmesan cheese, optional

Heat oven to 400 degrees. Line a baking sheet with parchment paper or aluminum foil. Place the cabbage steaks on the prepared baking sheet, leaving some space between each for even cooking. Brush the cabbage with the olive oil, coating thoroughly. Season the tops with salt, paprika, pepper, and thyme. Bake the cabbage steaks for about 35 minutes, until the leaves are browned and the center is tender. If adding Parmesan cheese, sprinkle it over the cabbage steaks after 25 minutes of baking.

Last of the Summer Vegetables Gratin

Serves 8

This is a signature dish for me. It's beautiful to serve and tastes fantastic no matter what combination of vegetables you use. The garden flavors with woodsy thyme and roasted onions and peppers burst through this dish. I like to overlap the vegetables in a circle, lining them up side by side until they are all packed in like a coiled snake.

3 tablespoons plus ¼ cup extra-virgin olive oil, divided

2½ cups sliced onions

1 red bell pepper, chopped

2 teaspoons kosher salt, divided

3 teaspoons fresh thyme leaves, divided

2 cloves garlic, minced or grated

1 large (or 2 small) zucchini or yellow squash, cut into ¼-inch rounds

1 Japanese eggplant (or other small, narrow eggplant), cut into ¼-inch rounds

4 Roma tomatoes, cut into ¼-inch rounds

freshly ground black pepper

½ cup grated Parmesan cheese

1 cup panko bread crumbs

Heat oven to 375 degrees. Heat 3 tablespoons of olive oil in a large skillet over medium heat. Add onions and bell pepper and sprinkle with 1 teaspoon salt and 2 teaspoons thyme. Cook for about 10 minutes, until the onions are translucent and the pepper is soft. Add garlic and cook for 2 minutes more.

In a large bowl, combine zucchini, eggplant, and tomatoes. Add remaining ¼ cup olive oil and toss to coat. Sprinkle with remaining 1 teaspoon salt and pepper and toss again.

In a small bowl, mix Parmesan, bread crumbs, and remaining 1 teaspoon thyme.

Spread onion and pepper mixture on the bottom of a 9-inch pie pan or a 10-inch cast iron skillet. Working in a spiral, make a row of overlapping zucchini, eggplant, and tomato slices. Sprinkle ½ cup of the cheese and bread crumb mixture over the row. Repeat with remaining vegetables, sprinkling with cheese-crumb mixture for each row. Sprinkle with salt and pepper to taste followed by the remaining cheese and bread crumb mixture. Drizzle any remaining oil from the bowl of vegetables on top of the gratin.

Bake for 1 hour, until the vegetables are softened and the top of the gratin is brown and bubbly. If desired, place gratin under the broiler for 3–5 minutes to finish browning.

Candied Brussels Sprouts

Serves 4

This side dish is killer, and everyone I make it for wants the recipe. The umami of the fish sauce and the saltiness of the peanuts are a perfect match. The sweetness from the sugar and the acid from the lime really put this dish over the top. The final sprinkling of fresh herbs finishes it off. Even the little kids will like it — just emphasize the "candied" part.

For sauce

½ cup fish sauce

½ cup water

¼ cup fresh lime juice

2 teaspoons chopped garlic

1 tablespoon sambal oelek

½ cup granulated sugar

½ teaspoon kosher salt

For brussels sprouts

1 tablespoon canola oil

1–1½ pounds brussels sprouts, halved or quartered if very large

½ cup chopped mint

2 tablespoons chopped cilantro

1 tablespoon chopped peanuts

Heat cast iron skillet to almost smoking, about 4 minutes. Meanwhile, add sauce ingredients to a Mason jar and shake to combine.

Add the canola oil to the heated pan and swirl to coat the pan completely, then add the brussels sprouts. Shake the skillet to get as many of the sprouts cut side down as possible. Let them sit undisturbed for 5 minutes or until they develop a dark brown caramelized surface. Stir the sprouts and add the sauce. Continue cooking for 3–4 minutes, until the sprouts are caramelized and the sauce is more of a sticky glaze.

Remove from the heat and add to a serving dish. Top with the mint, cilantro, and peanuts.

Roast Savory Pork Shoulder with Mustard, Rosemary, Thyme, and Sage on Polenta

Serves 8

Pork shoulder is one of my favorite meats. This recipe involves slow cooking in a Dutch oven with mustard, beer, and lots of fresh herbs, but I also cook the shoulder in a variety of other ways. In the hot summer months, I cook pork shoulder on the grill in a baking dish covered with aluminum foil, then serve it pulled for barbecue sandwiches. In the fall, I cook it in the slow cooker for tacos. This recipe is great in the winter to warm up the whole house.

For pork

1 (6-pound) bone-in pork shoulder

1 teaspoon kosher salt, plus more to taste

1 teaspoon freshly ground black pepper, plus more to taste

⅓ cup Dijon mustard

¼ cup finely chopped fresh sage

1 tablespoon finely chopped fresh thyme leaves

1 tablespoon finely chopped fresh rosemary leaves

4 cloves garlic, minced

2 cups sliced yellow onions

1 tablespoon extra-virgin olive oil

1 bottle beer (choose an IPA, like Bent Paddle)

1 cup chicken broth

1 tablespoon unsalted butter

For polenta

5 cups whole milk

3 cups water

2 cups polenta (medium-ground cornmeal)

1 cup heavy cream

2 cups finely grated Parmesan cheese

½ cup (1 stick) unsalted butter

2 tablespoons kosher salt

freshly cracked black pepper, to taste

For pork

Heat oven to 325 degrees. Season pork with salt and pepper. Use your hands to spread mustard over pork. Sprinkle with sage, thyme, rosemary, and garlic and rub all over the roast to coat. Place onions in a Dutch oven. Season with salt, pepper, and olive oil and toss. Place the roast on top of the onions and pour in the beer. Roast the pork, basting with pan juices about every hour, until the pork is well browned and very tender, about 5 hours.

For polenta

In a medium saucepan over medium-high heat, bring milk and water to a boil. Reduce heat to medium. Gradually add the polenta, whisking constantly, then bring to a simmer. Reduce heat to low, cover pan, and cook, whisking every 10 minutes, for 30 minutes or until the polenta is cooked and creamy. Remove from heat and add cream, Parmesan cheese, butter, salt, and pepper. Whisk until butter and cheese are melted and polenta is the consistency of cake batter or a bit thicker.

For serving

Remove pork to a plate. Add a cup or so of chicken broth to the juices in the pan and stir with a whisk to scrape up any browned bits. Season with salt and pepper to taste and stir in butter for a glossy, rich sauce.

Pull the roasted pork into large chunks. Pour the polenta onto a platter and top with roasted pork pieces. Drizzle some of the pan juices over the meat and serve the rest alongside.

Tomato Pie

Serves 10

The first time I had tomato pie was at my friend Sue Jacob's house. Sue is a prolific gardener and a fantastic baker. Her tomato pie was the first savory pie I ever had, and I remember how impressed I was and how good it tasted. The simplicity of the ingredients really lets the garden tomatoes shine. The mustard at the bottom of the pie acts as insulation from the tomato juices, allowing you to get a crisp crust. Experiment with the cheese — mozzarella, Swiss, Parmesan, Gruyère, or a mix. Let the pie rest a minimum of 30 minutes for the juices and cheese to set before you cut into it.

For crust

1¼ cups all-purpose flour

½ teaspoon kosher salt

1 teaspoon fresh thyme leaves

½ cup (1 stick) unsalted butter, cut into ½-inch cubes

3 tablespoons ice water

1 tablespoon vodka

For filling

⅓ cup Dijon mustard

2 cups grated Gruyère cheese, divided

3 large ripe tomatoes, thinly sliced

1 tablespoon chopped fresh thyme leaves

1 tablespoon extra-virgin olive oil

1 teaspoon kosher salt

freshly cracked black pepper

For crust

Add flour, salt, and thyme to a food processor. Pulse 2 to 3 times, until combined. Scatter the butter cubes over the flour and pulse 4 to 5 times, until flour is evenly distributed. The dough should look crumbly. Add ice water through the tube of the food processor, pulsing once after each tablespoon. The crumbs should begin to form larger clusters. Add the vodka and continue to pulse until the dough comes together in a ball and awkwardly spins in the machine.

Remove dough from bowl and place in a mound on a clean surface. Work the dough just enough to form a ball. Flatten to a disk, wrap in plastic wrap, and refrigerate at least 30 minutes or up to 2 days before making the tomato pie.

To assemble

Heat oven to 375 degrees. Roll out a 12-inch dough circle to ¼ inch thick. Lay the crust in a 9-inch pie pan and fold the extra dough over the edges to create a double thick wall. Spread the bottom of the crust with mustard, sprinkle with half the cheese, and cover with tomato slices. Sprinkle the rest of the cheese on top of the tomato slices. Sprinkle fresh thyme and drizzle olive oil over the top of the pie. Sprinkle salt and freshly cracked black pepper over the assembled pie.

Bake for about 30 minutes. Let rest 30 minutes before slicing. Serve warm or at room temperature.

Cherry Tomato and Garlic Baked Rice

Serves 6

This recipe, adapted from Yotam Otto-lenghi's *Simple: A Cookbook*, uses lots of cherry tomatoes and a whole bulb of garlic, which seems like too much but works when it's all baked down. Like all of Ottolenghi's dishes, this one looks very beautiful and rustic, with colorful bursts of tomato that pop in your mouth.

2 pounds (about 50) cherry tomatoes

1 garlic bulb, peeled and roughly chopped into bite-size pieces

1 cup chopped yellow onion

⅓ cup chopped cilantro stems

6 tablespoons chopped cilantro leaves, divided

3 tablespoons fresh thyme leaves

½ cup extra-virgin olive oil

1 teaspoon kosher salt, divided

freshly cracked black pepper

1½ cups basmati rice

2½ cups boiling water

Heat oven to 350 degrees. Arrange the tomatoes, garlic, onion, cilantro stems, 5 tablespoons cilantro leaves, and thyme in a large (8x12–inch), high-sided casserole dish. Drizzle the olive oil over the vegetables, add ½ teaspoon salt and a good grind of black pepper. Bake for 1 hour, until the vegetables are soft. Remove from the oven, sprinkle the rice evenly over the vegetables without stirring, and set aside.

Increase the oven temperature to 450 degrees. Sprinkle remaining ½ teaspoon salt and plenty of black pepper over the rice and then carefully pour the boiling water over the rice. Seal the dish tightly with foil and place in the oven for 25 minutes, until the rice is cooked. Remove from the oven and set aside for 10 minutes, still covered.

Remove the foil, gently stir in remaining 1 tablespoon cilantro leaves, and serve.

Warm Bacon Potato Salad

Serves 4-6

Warm bacon potato salad is a staple in German households. Potatoes dressed in apple cider vinaigrette and mustard with salty crumbled bacon give this dish a savory punch that's welcome after a summer of heavy mayonnaise-based potato salads.

For vinaigrette

3 cloves garlic, minced or grated

⅓ cup apple cider vinegar

1 tablespoon extra-virgin olive oil

1 tablespoon Dijon mustard

2 teaspoons kosher salt

1 teaspoon black pepper

1 teaspoon granulated sugar

For salad

6 medium Yukon Gold potatoes

4 strips bacon

1 cup chopped red onion

2 tablespoons chopped fresh dill

2 tablespoons chopped Italian flat-leaf parsley

freshly cracked black pepper

For vinaigrette

Add ingredients to a Mason jar and shake until thoroughly combined.

For salad

Place potatoes in a pot of cold water. Bring to a boil and cook for about 15 minutes or until fork tender. Drain. When cool, chop into rough 1-inch chunks and set aside.

In a cast iron skillet, cook the bacon until crisp. Remove slices to a paper towel–lined plate to cool; then crumble and set aside. Add red onions to bacon grease in the skillet, and cook over medium heat until tender, about 5 minutes. Add potatoes to the skillet and heat through, about 5 minutes.

Transfer onion and potato mixture to a serving bowl. Add crumbled bacon and toss with the vinaigrette, dill, and parsley. Add freshly cracked black pepper to finish.

Spicy Pumpkin Seed Brittle

Serves 12

Every year for our holiday cookie exchange, I try to mix up the recipe I bring. Cranberry-orange or lemon–poppy seed bread, peppermint meringues, caramels, and frosted sugar cookies are all recipes I've done, but this spicy pumpkin seed brittle was a personal favorite. Though I've made this for the holidays, it's of course great in the fall for a book club or Halloween gathering.

1 cup granulated sugar

⅓ cup corn syrup

3 tablespoons water

3 tablespoons unsalted butter

1 cup raw pumpkin seeds

1 teaspoon baking soda

1 teaspoon kosher salt

½ teaspoon ground cinnamon

¼ teaspoon cayenne

Set a nonstick silicone baking mat on your counter or work space.

In a medium saucepan over medium heat, bring sugar, corn syrup, and water to a boil, stirring to dissolve sugar, about 3 minutes. Adjust the heat to medium low and continue to stir until the sugar has become a light golden-brown color, about 12 minutes more. Add the butter and allow it to melt, then add the pumpkin seeds. Cook, stirring constantly, until golden brown, about 3 minutes. Add the baking soda, salt, cinnamon, and cayenne and stir for 1 minute more.

Pour the mixture onto the baking mat and allow the brittle to come to room temperature until completely hardened. Break into pieces.

Apple Skillet Cake with Salted Caramel Sauce

Serves 8

Baking in a ten-inch cast iron skillet is always a favorite at the cabin. My cast iron is seasoned perfectly from years of use, and I love how it looks when serving this apple cake. The salted caramel sauce is fantastic. For years I avoided any recipe that called for making caramel sauce: I was afraid the goo would bubble up and boil over and I'd ruin it (and make a huge mess). No more! If *I* can make caramel sauce, so can you, and this sauce with this cake is a perfect pairing.

For cake

1½ cups all-purpose flour

1 tablespoon baking powder

1 teaspoon kosher salt

3 teaspoons ground cinnamon, divided

3 large eggs

1 cup plus 1 tablespoon granulated sugar, divided

½ cup packed brown sugar

⅓ cup plain Greek yogurt

⅓ cup vegetable oil

1 teaspoon vanilla extract

4 cups Honeycrisp apples, peeled, cored, chopped into ½-inch cubes

½ cup chopped walnuts, toasted

For caramel

1½ cups granulated sugar

½ cup (1 stick) plus 1 tablespoon unsalted butter, cut into cubes

¾ cup heavy cream, at room temperature

2 teaspoons kosher salt

For cake

Heat oven to 350 degrees. Grease and flour a 10-inch cast iron skillet. In a medium bowl, mix flour, baking soda, salt, and 2 teaspoons cinnamon. Set aside.

In a large bowl of a stand mixer, combine eggs, 1 cup granulated sugar, and brown sugar, mixing for 5 minutes. Add yogurt, oil, and vanilla, and blend until combined. Add dry mixture to the wet and mix well. Fold in apples and nuts. Pour batter into the prepared cast iron skillet.

In a small bowl, mix remaining 1 tablespoon sugar with remaining 1 teaspoon cinnamon. Sprinkle mixture over the cake. Bake for 45 minutes or until a toothpick inserted into the center comes out clean.

For caramel

Place the sugar in a medium saucepan on medium-high heat and stir constantly with a whisk until sugar melts into an amber-colored liquid and no clumps remain. This typically takes 6–8 minutes.

At the amber liquid stage, reduce the heat to medium. Carefully add each cube of butter (mixture will bubble up and foam) and continue whisking until all the butter is fully melted and incorporated. Add the cream in a steady stream while continually whisking the sugar and butter mixture. As soon as the cream is incorporated, increase the heat to medium high and let the caramel come to a boil for 1 full minute before removing it from the heat. Stir in the salt. The caramel will thicken as it cools.

Serve drizzled over the cake slices.

Double Chocolate Zucchini Bread

Serves 10

This loaf looks beautiful, and the dark chocolate flavor is superb, while the zucchini keeps the cake moist. I made this chocolate bread with Lemony Zucchini Bread (page 153) and served both for daughter Ellie's birthday one year. I picked up two loaf pans for two dollars each at the Ely secondhand store. The loaves were a hit!

1¼ cups all-purpose flour

⅓ cup granulated sugar

¼ cup cocoa powder

1½ teaspoons baking powder

1½ teaspoons baking soda

1 teaspoon ground cinnamon

½ teaspoon nutmeg

½ teaspoon kosher salt

2 large eggs

½ cup 2 percent milk

¼ cup plain Greek yogurt

4 tablespoons butter, melted

1 teaspoon vanilla extract

1⅓ cups zucchini grated on a box grater

1 (10-ounce) package bittersweet dark chocolate baking chunks, ¼ cup reserved for sprinkling

Heat oven to 350 degrees. Prepare an 8x4–inch loaf pan with nonstick spray.

In a medium bowl, combine the flour, sugar, cocoa powder, baking powder, baking soda, cinnamon, nutmeg, and salt.

In a large bowl, whisk together the eggs, milk, yogurt, butter, and vanilla. Stir in the zucchini. Add the dry ingredients to the wet ingredients and stir until just combined. Do not overmix. Fold in the chocolate chips, reserving ¼ cup.

Pour the batter into the loaf pan. Sprinkle with reserved chocolate chips and bake for 45–50 minutes, or until a toothpick inserted into the center comes out clean. Remove from the oven and cool completely.

# The Perfect Apple Pie

Serves 8-10

Each year I make a New Year's resolution around food. Typically, it involves a technique I want to learn, like making sourdough bread (hello, pandemic bakers of 2020), or making the perfect apple pie. One year, I took a pie class from an excellent local baker (@heathers_pies on Instagram) and learned her pie crust secret (hello, vodka!).

For crust

2½ cups all-purpose flour

1 teaspoon kosher salt

1 cup (2 sticks) unsalted butter, cut into ½-inch cubes

4 tablespoons ice water

2 tablespoons vodka

1 large egg white plus 1 teaspoon water, for egg wash

For filling

6 medium Granny Smith apples, peeled, halved, cored, cut into ¼-inch slices

2 teaspoons fresh lemon juice

⅔ cup packed light brown sugar

¼ cup plus 1 tablespoon granulated sugar

3 tablespoons cornstarch

1 teaspoon ground cinnamon, plus more to taste

1 teaspoon kosher salt

½ teaspoon ground nutmeg

1 tablespoon cold butter, cubed

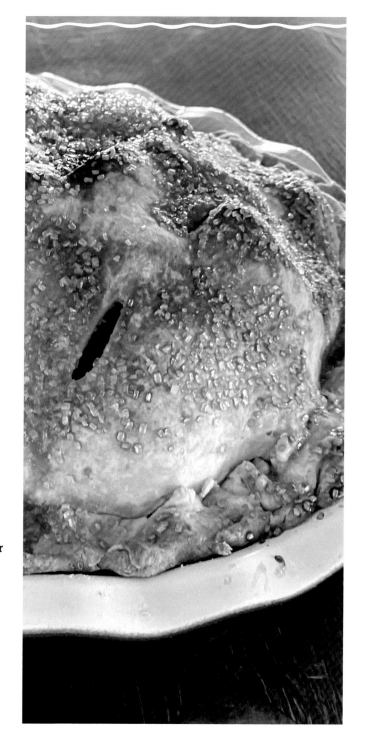

For crust

Add flour and salt to a food processor. Pulse 2 to 3 times, until combined. Scatter butter cubes over flour and pulse 4 to 5 times, until flour is evenly distributed. Dough should look crumbly. Add ice water, a tablespoon at a time, through the tube, pulsing once after each addition. The crumbs should begin to form larger clusters. Add the vodka and continue to pulse until the dough comes together in a ball and awkwardly spins in the machine.

Remove dough from bowl and place in a mound on a clean surface. Work the dough just enough to form a ball. Divide in half, then flatten each half into a disk. Wrap each disk with plastic wrap and refrigerate at least 1 hour and up to 2 days (in a pinch, freeze dough for 30 minutes).

On a lightly floured surface, roll out 1 dough disk to a 15-inch round about ⅛ inch thick. Carefully press the dough into a pie dish. Place the lined pie dish in the freezer and make the filling.

For filling

Put the apples in a large bowl and add lemon juice, brown sugar, ¼ cup granulated sugar, cornstarch, cinnamon, salt, and nutmeg. Toss to coat well.

To assemble and bake

Heat oven to 425 degrees. On a lightly floured surface, roll out second dough disk to a 15-inch round about ⅛ inch thick. Mound the filling in the pie plate, rearranging the fruit as needed to make the pile compact. Dot the apples with the cold butter cubes. Add top crust and fold edges of the top crust underneath edges of the bottom crust, pressing to seal and creating a thicker, ¼-inch border. If dough rises above the lip of the dish, try to make it uniform all the way around. Crimp edges with a fork or press together with fingers. Freeze the assembled pie for 10 minutes before baking.

Just before baking, take the pie from the freezer and make an egg wash by whisking 1 egg white and 1 teaspoon water in a small bowl. Brush egg wash over the top crust. Sprinkle egg wash with remaining 1 tablespoon sugar. Cut 4 slits on top of the pie to vent.

Place a rimmed baking sheet or an aluminum foil drip pan on the lower oven rack to catch any juices that overflow during baking. Set the pie on the rack above.

Bake until the top and bottom crusts are golden and the juices are bubbling, about 1 hour. Listen for the bubbling, which means the fruit has broken down. If the pie is browning too quickly, cover the edges with a premade foil shield (see tip). During the last 5 minutes of baking, remove the foil tent. Cool the pie at least 3 hours to let the juices firm up before serving.

TIP: To make the shield, fold a 12-inch square piece of foil into quarters. With scissors, cut out the center to make a 2-inch-wide ring that will shield your crust edges while baking.

Chas's Homemade Granola

Serves 12-15

Chas (Charles McKhann II) grew up in the seventies with my husband, Kurt, and he and his family have been our close friends for years. They recently moved from Walla Walla, Washington, to the small community of Cornucopia, Wisconsin, on the south shore of Lake Superior. Chas is brilliant, sarcastic, thoughtful, and a great friend with a head of hair that rivals Fabio and a Burt Reynolds/Tom Selleck pornstache right out of the seventies. The mustache is big, bushy, sexy, and right at home on my friend Chas's face. In addition to being a college professor, he's also a hippie who, along with his sister, Lisa, spent many summers at Burntside Lake camping, canoeing, and joining us for meals at True North Island. So, who better than an old hippie professor with a pornstache to supply their not-so-secret recipe for granola? I like this recipe because of the natural ingredients. You can find most of them at Zup's in Ely or at the natural food store in town, Organic Roots. This granola has it all — the sweetness of honey, coconut, and molasses, healthy chia seeds, and the crunch from a quick bake that brings it all together. Chas eats his granola with milk, but I eat it plain by the handful.

1½ cups water

⅓ cup flax seeds

1 cup slivered almonds

1 cup pumpkin seeds

8 cups rolled oats

1 cup shredded unsweetened coconut

1 cup vegetable oil

1 cup honey

⅓ cup molasses

1 cup dried tart cherries

Heat oven to 300 degrees. Spray 2 large, rimmed baking sheets with cooking spray. In a small saucepan, bring water to a boil and add flax seeds. Simmer for 5 minutes or until flax seeds burst open and get goopy. Set aside.

In a dry cast iron skillet over medium heat, toast slivered almonds and pumpkin seeds until browned and fragrant, stirring occasionally, about 2–5 minutes. (Note: These burn quickly so tend them at all times.)

In a large bowl, mix oats, coconut, and toasted almonds and pumpkin seeds. In a medium bowl, mix vegetable oil, honey, molasses, and flax seed goop. Add the wet ingredients to the dry and stir well to coat all the pieces. Divide and spread granola mix evenly between prepared baking sheets.

Bake for about 1 hour, turning pans around and switching the pans from top to bottom every 15 minutes for even cooking. Let the pans cool thoroughly, until granola becomes hard and crispy. Crumble cooled granola into a large bowl and mix in cherries. Store in an airtight container.

Cabin Caramel Corn

Makes approximately 8 cups

Watching me eat popcorn is a horror show. I shovel it in by the handful, I spill it everywhere, and I've been banned from sharing popcorn with my daughter, Ellie, at the movies. When we want something sweet after dinner, caramel corn is a cabin classic because we always have the ingredients on hand. This recipe makes enough for four people — or one hungry popcorn-eating savage like me.

2 tablespoons vegetable oil

¼ cup popping corn kernels

4 tablespoons butter

¼ cup brown sugar

1 teaspoon kosher salt

Heat the oil in a 3-quart, thick-bottomed saucepan on medium-high heat. Add the popping corn and cover, then wait for it to pop, about 1 minute, with a few more minutes of vigorous popping until the pops slow down. Remove pan from heat and pour popped corn into a paper grocery bag.

Melt the butter in the same saucepan on medium-high heat and add the sugar, constantly mixing with a spatula. Let it boil until the caramel is a golden color. Remove from the heat and pour caramel over the popcorn. Add the salt and shake the bag to mix. Taste and adjust seasonings, adding more salt if necessary.

Dolores's Shortbread Cookies

Makes about 24 cookies

The *True North Cabin Cookbook* exists only because of my mother-in-law, Dolores Johnson. Dolores was in her forties when her husband, Richard, died of lung cancer. Unfortunately, Richard left little savings behind, and True North Island still had a mortgage. Dolores, who had recently become a stay-at-home mother, went back to work, eventually rising to managing director of the Houston Grand Opera. She kept up the mortgage on the island and paid for the upkeep, the boats, and the taxes while her young adult children pursued burgeoning careers. The island became the ancestral home, so to speak, where the far-flung family members could meet every summer.

Dolores and I have spent many summers together in the kitchen at True North Island. Dolores would get up before me, put on her white terry cloth robe, make coffee, and read the *New York Times* on her iPad. Then when I'd come into the kitchen, the evening meal discussion would commence. Once the meal was set, we would find out if we had the ingredients on the island or if we needed to take the boat to the marina to the car to town. That's how our days began: figuring out what we were having for dinner and who was coming to eat. We've had so many beautiful True North Island dinners with family and guests, cocktails, toasts, wine, food, more wine, and dessert. When it was just Dolores, Kurt, and me, Kurt would often do the dishes after dinner, and Dolores and I would sit with one more glass of wine and enjoy the evening's final bit of light.

Dolores found her shortbread cookie recipe in the dog-eared paperback copy of the *Fannie Farmer Cookbook* in our cabin kitchen. She initially made the cookies for her first grandchild, Brittany, who loved shortbread. The original recipe was written by Marion Cunningham, a contemporary of Julia Child and James Beard, who wrote dozens of cookbooks. Dolores cuts her shortbread into diamond shapes, and they're each dotted with a fork in even intervals. She stores the cookies in an old, slanted Mason cookie jar with a rubber-sealed lid. I remember her baking the shortbread cookies inside the cabin on a sweltering eighty-five-degree day because Brittany would soon arrive.

For me, Dolores's simple shortbread cookies epitomize True North Island, the place we all share and love each summer. As the island became the ancestral home of Kurt, Kristi, and Erik, it too has become my home. Brittany, Sylvie, Charlie, Mellissa, Anna, Dominic, Christopher, Michelle, Grace, babies Wyatt, Ollie, and Sophia, and hopefully Ellie and her children will all make it their ancestral home too and honor our memories and family time on True North Island.

I love you, Dolores. Thanks for all the time on True North Island. Thanks for the family memories, from the shore lunches and campfires at the point to the picnics and pontoon rides and, of course, all those meals at our dinner table overlooking Burntside Lake.

1 cup (2 sticks) unsalted
    butter, softened

½ cup confectioners' sugar

2 cups all-purpose flour

½ teaspoon kosher salt

¼ teaspoon baking powder

Heat oven to 350 degrees. Mix the
butter until creamy, then gradually add
the sugar, beating well. In a separate
bowl, mix together the flour, salt, and
baking powder. Add dry ingredients
to the butter and sugar mixture, com-
bining thoroughly.

Use a rolling pin to roll out the dough to
¼ inch thick, then cut into rectangles or
other desired shape. Place on ungreased
baking sheets, prick each cookie with
a fork, and bake for 20–25 minutes or
until lightly browned around the edges.

Acknowledgments

This book started as a dream of cataloging our families' cabin recipes and became a reality with the help of my husband, Kurt Johnson. With plenty of time on my hands during the COVID-19 pandemic, I said I wanted to write a cookbook. Kurt helped with the query letter, and he encouraged me, inspired me, edited the pages, and tutored me throughout this process while simultaneously publishing his first novel, *The Barrens*, cowritten with our daughter, Ellie Johnson.

Thanks to all the Johnsons, Jacobs, Hansens, Jacobsons, Collins, Barghinnis, and Leers who contributed stories, recipes, and a few photographs for this book. Thanks for eating all the food we prepared in the making of this cookbook. Special thanks to Dolores Johnson for the legacy of Johnson Island (True North), and for entertaining and cooking with me and always agreeing to have that last glass of wine at our island table while Kurt did the dishes.

Thanks to the Stephanies: Stephanie March, my radio partner at MyTalk 107.1, for spending every Saturday for fifteen years talking about food with me. Our conversations deepened my love for food, cooking, travel, and Minnesota makers, inspiring me to write this cookbook. And Stephanie Bloomquist, thank you for your support on stephaniesdish.com and for your guidance and editing expertise throughout this cookbook.

Thanks to Shannon Pennefeather for your editing skills and the Minnesota Historical Society Press staff for helping this project come to fruition.

Lastly, thanks, Mom. You never made it to the island, but I believe all those years watching you cubing potatoes for potato salad, whisking gravy, and frying chicken started me on my way.

K. Solberg Photography

ABOUT THE AUTHOR

Stephanie Hansen grew up in the Twin Cities, where one of her first forays into the food life was a job wearing a poodle skirt, dancing on bar tops, and slinging drinks at the Heartthrob Café in downtown St. Paul. While the gig was fun, the hours were crappy and she got tired of smelling like a bar.

Hansen worked for the next fifteen years in print, radio, and direct mail advertising sales and marketing. In 2005 she started her own online printing and marketing company, Printz.com. Fast-forward eight years, and she won the Woman Business Owner of the Year Award. Fast-forward another three years, and she sold the thriving business for a large pile of cash and thought she would retire at forty-two. Turns out the pile of cash wasn't that large and retirement was boring, so she leaned in to her love of food and her burgeoning life as a broadcaster.

Hansen is cohost of *Weekly Dish* radio show and podcast on Hubbard Broadcasting's myTalk107.1 with *Mpls.St.Paul Magazine* food editor Stephanie March. Hansen also produces and hosts the *Makers of Minnesota* podcast, on which food is a favorite topic. And she talks with other food writers, cookbook authors, and fans of food on her podcast *Dishing with Stephanie's Dish*. Hansen cooks and shares recipes weekly on *The Jason Show* on KMSP Fox 9 in the Twin Cities. Learn more at StephaniesDish.com.

Hansen loves to travel and has sailed throughout the Caribbean, Italy, and Croatia. She relishes #vanlife in her Winnebago Paseo and is a summer resident of Ely, Minnesota, spending time on Burntside Lake, where she wrote and photographed *True North Cabin Cookbook*.